Pressing Your Own Buttons

PANIC!

Take Control of Your Life So Others Don't! ™

Gary Screaton Page, Ph.D.

Publisher Data and Legal Information

Published by Gary Screaton Page.

Illustrations by Mike F. Kicul

Cover Design by Gary Screaton Page.

Contact the Publisher at:
URL:http://www.garyscreatonpage.com
Email:garypage@garyscreatonpage.com

ISBN: 978-0-9733872-8-5

Disclaimer

The author has changed the names and identifying characteristics of people alluded to in this book, and he does not intend to refer to specific persons. All situations are simulations of those encountered in practice and the names do not refer to actual persons involved but are composites of people with whom the author may have worked. Any resemblance, then, to an identifiable person is coincidental and unintended.

The author has made what he believes to be reasonable efforts to use illustrations that he specifically and privately commissioned, or he believes to be legitimately from public domain sources. Please, notify the author of any oversights so he can either fairly compensate the creator of them and/or remove them from future editions. The author regrets any oversight and, if there are any, they were unintentional.

This publication contains the opinions and ideas of its author. It is intended to provide helpful and informative material on the subjects addressed in the publication. It is sold with the understanding that neither the author nor the publisher are engaged in rendering medical, health, or any other kind of personal professional services in these learning materials. The reader should consult his or her medical, health, or other competent professional before adopting any of the suggestions in these resources or drawing inferences from them.

The author and publisher specifically disclaim all responsibility for any liability, loss, or risk, personal or otherwise, which is incurred as a consequence, directly or indirectly, of the use and/or application of any of the contents of this book.

Gary Screaton Page, Ph.D.

DEDICATION

No book is the result of the effort of just one person. Others are always involved. At the top of the list of those who made this book possible is Dr. Clifford Christensen. "Cliff," as most of his students knew him, was Department Chair when I had the good fortune to have him for my Psychology Professor at the Ontario Institute of Education (O.I.S.E.) in Toronto, Ontario, Canada. He was a caring, insightful, encouraging, and good-natured taskmaster who challenged me to think creatively. When he agreed to be my Thesis Advisor, I could not have been more fortunate. He helped me focus and to believe the work was worth the effort. This book and the related learning resources are the direct result of the research of Dr. Christensen and the contributions of those who worked with him [1] as he developed the model presented here.

In a very real way, Cliff Christensen and his team are the lead authors of this book and I its co-author. I will always be grateful to Cliff for giving me permission to take his research and publications and to develop them into the present work and the companion Programmed Workbook. Together with the audio and video material, they form a self-instructional system to help every reader become a more effective person. I have built this book and the companion Workbook and audio-visual materials upon *Development and Field-testing of an Interpersonal Coping Skills Program*. In 1974, Dr. Christensen, and others [2] in the Department of Applied Psychology at the Ontario Institute for Studies in Education, published the original work. The foundation of this book is the work done through Research and Development Project Number 812.

Due to Dr. Christensen's encouragement and direction while I was his student, I was able to complete the two volumes that make up the *Pressing Your Own Buttons: Take Control of Your Life So Others Don't!* ™ counseling system. In his honor, a portion of all proceeds from the sale of each of the volumes and related resources will go to a scholarship named in his honor. The scholarship will go to a Psychology Student in the O.I.S.E. Graduate School at the University of Toronto.

Cliff, I thank you for being you and for teaching me that I *can* press my own buttons!

Gary Screaton Page, Ph.D.

TABLE OF CONTENTS

Preface

This book will liberate you! ***Pressing Your Own Buttons: Take Control of Your Life So Others Don't***™ will help you gain a fuller understanding of yourself and others. What is more, you will be freer to act and to take control of all your relationships. By the time you finish this book (***Pressing Your Own Buttons***™ for short), <u>you can be the person you want to be</u>.

Where Are We Going?

No one is an island. Humans need to interact with other people. Who and what we are at any given point in our lives, is a result of what we learn ourselves, or either directly or indirectly from other people. You see, our brains are like digital recorders. All our life experiences pass through our brains. Some of those experiences stay in our short-term memories for, well, a short time. Others, our brains record, and they stay there for our lifetimes. Some of those experiences are positive and helpful, and even can be life saving. Other experiences are negative. Over time, they may prove not to be helpful at all.

The significant people in our lives affect us considerably, often for good, but not always so. By what they say, do, and by how they look they make impressions on the digital recorders that are our brains. It's as if the behavior of others presses our "Record" **REC** buttons, and what they say, do, or how they look is stored there. Later, similar people that remind us of what we heard and saw our significant others say, do, or how they looked, press our "Play" buttons, and we may play back these recordings. If the experiences are positive, we continue to "listen" and attend.

At other times, however, the recordings that we play back are negative. The people that remind us of them seem to press our "Stop" or "Pause" buttons. What they say, do, or how they look, make us hesitant and cautious and may even make us so tense we seem unable to function at all in their presence. There are also times when the behavior of other people presses our

"Rewind" or "Fast Forward" buttons. We want to avoid altogether, the memories and feelings these people generate in us.

Still, other times we don't like what others say, do, or how they look. Then we may want to change it. These people "press" our "Rewind" and "Record" buttons. We try to "record over" what they said, did, or how they looked and give new meaning to those things.

In each of these situations, we are reacting impulsively, automatically, and often irrationally. We are responding to those things that our significant others—parents, friends, bosses, teachers, siblings, among others—did or said, or to how they looked often years ago. We may not even be conscious of those experiences, "recorded" in our brains yet they continue to affect us so powerfully now.

Sound familiar? Of course it does. Like the rest of us, you have had experiences like that. Think how much better you would feel if you could take control and make instead a reasoned and rational response. Then you, not others, would be pressing your buttons— the buttons you choose. For instance, you could rationally decide to rewind the old recording, press your "Record" button, and lay down a completely new track by recording new thoughts over the old memories. You would then be able to *"Take Control of Your Life So Others Don't!"*™

You see, whenever we try to avoid, change, or tense in the presence of the troublesome behavior of others, we put them in control of us. In effect, we give them permission to press our buttons! As long as the speech, actions, and/or appearance of others control our behavior, we are no longer free to be the people we want to be.

That is why I created the *Pressing Your Own Buttons: Take Control of Your Life So Others Don't!*™. This book will liberate

3

you! Once you master the skills I'll teach you and you apply them, you'll be free to act the way *you* want. You'll no longer react like a robot to whatever others say, do, or to how they look. Instead, you'll have more control over your life. What's more, when you've completed the book you'll be able to help others become more effective, too. What you learn here will enrich your life and the lives of those you love.

There is nothing mysterious or difficult about what you'll be learning. You're quite capable of mastering every part. In fact, by the time you finish the book you'll know as much about it as I do. You'll be well on your way to becoming all that you want to be.

Now, let me take a few moments to tell you about the format of the **Pressing Your Own Buttons**™ counseling system of which this book is the key. Each chapter or lesson of this total learning system consists of three parts: the material you are reading now, an optional *PowerPoint®* audio-video presentation, and an optional *Programmed Workbook*.

I have designed each part of this training system to take you on a journey of self-discovery. Along the way, you'll discover the "hot buttons" in your life. You'll also learn how to stop other people from pressing them.

Together, this *Manual*, the *PowerPoint® Audio/Video* material, and the *Programmed Workbook*, form a powerful training partnership. Be clear, **the *Manual* alone will give you a good understanding of the process, and enable you to make meaningful changes in your life.** Using all three components together will maximize the benefits you get from the total learning system. Reading, listening, and doing are more effective working together, than any one of them alone.

Many people feel more comfortable reading the *Manual*. Others feel they learn better; when they review material and test their knowledge with the *Programmed Workbook.* Still others choose to use the complete system: each format reinforcing the others. The choice is yours and the **Pressing Your Own Buttons™** *Manual* is an excellent start. After all, you are already beginning to make rational decisions and learning to **Take Control of Your Life So Others Don't!™**

If you do want to have your personal copies of either, or both, the Programmed Workbook or the *PowerPoint®* Audio/Video resource, go to www.pressingyourownbuttons.com. You can get the whole package for an affordable investment of less than the cost of just one coaching or therapy session.

Much research and writing went into the **Pressing Your Own Buttons™** learning system. I developed the system and tested its effectiveness so it can guide you through the entire **Pressing Your Own Buttons™** program in the privacy of your own home.

Studies[3] have consistently shown that the programmed instructional format, used in the Workbook, is very effective for learning new material. I know of no more cost-effective way to help you master this program. This *Manual, Programmed Workbook, and the PowerPoint® Audio-Video Presentation together* form a training system that will enable you to take control of your life and release you to be all that you can be.

All components of the **Pressing Your Own Buttons™** learning system (the Manual, Workbook, and audio/visual materials, have the same nine lessons as follows:

1. The Beginning of Wisdom.

2. Discovering YOUR "Hot Buttons"

3. Observation, Inference, and Evaluation.

4. How Do You Know That What They Said Is What You Thought They Meant?

5. Who's Pressing Your Buttons?

6. Where Did THAT Come From?

7. Cooling Your "Hot Buttons".

8. Feelings, Emotions, and Actions: What You Don't Know Will Surprise You!

9. The "Hot Buttons" Within.

Reinforcing Activities

Throughout **Pressing Your Own Buttons**™ you'll find several short activities to try. They reinforce the concepts you'll learn. Each activity will provide you with an opportunity to have some direct experience with the important ideas covered in the program. These ideas and concepts will enable you to act more freely at home, work, or anywhere you might find yourself in the company of others.

Think of these activities, as miniature experiments in which you can try out the skills you will be learning. Doing these activities, will help you to discover for yourself many effective ways of communicating and working with others. Each activity is itself the result of careful research and forms an integral part of the **Pressing Your Own Buttons**™ approach. Doing them as directed will help to insure your success with the program.

Complete each lesson of the book, apply what you learn, and you will be free to be all you can be. No longer will anyone press your buttons without your permission. By the end of this book, you will be able to *"Take control of your life so other don't!"*™

Chapter 1:

The Beginning of Wisdom

Let's get you started ***Pressing Your Own Buttons***™. By investing in this eBook, you have already shown your desire to grow in your understanding of yourself and others, and in your effectiveness as a responsible, independent person. I believe you will find the ideas interesting, easy to learn, practical, and above all, helpful.

At this point, you may be asking, "What have I gotten myself into?" Let me begin by saying, right up front, that some of what I will tell you may not be clear to you at first. Don't be too concerned about that right now. I'll explain things as we go along. I know it's important for you to understand what you're doing.

There is nothing mysterious about ***Pressing Your Own Buttons***™. Without question, you are quite capable of understanding the process. In fact, I expect that by the end of the program you'll know just as much as I do. You'll readily be able to use the ideas yourself. What is more, it's quite possible you will use what you learn to help others who are up tight or troubled in some way. Of book, you will not become a qualified counselor just because you have mastered this system. My attorney insists I make that quite clear. You would need years of training to become a therapist of any kind.

Central to everything in this system you are about to learn, is the fact that other people's behavior affects us. For example, if someone shouts angry words at us we might choose to shout back. Alternatively, we might choose to walk away. If they greet us cheerfully, we might feel happy and smile back.

John, a participant in one of our **Pressing Your Own Buttons Boot Camps**™, said he was unable to tolerate his girlfriend being sad or crying. Here's what happened during that session. See how the leader — <u>for fun</u> I've called him "Sigmund" — handled John's situation.[4]

Now, let's eavesdrop on Sigmund's group, already in progress.

"Now, then, consider John's example," Sigmund began after the group's short break. "John said that he became very uncomfortable when his girlfriend cried ... or even if it just looked like she might cry. John, do you mind telling us what you did when your girlfriend cried? Think back to the last time that she cried. Try to get an image or picture of her crying. Tell us what led up to it. Tell us *exactly* what you said and did."

Hesitating at first, perhaps collecting his thoughts, John spoke softly, "Last time she cried because I said that I was going camping with the guys. I remember I tried not to look at her. Actually, I would have preferred to tell her on the telephone because I knew what would happen. Well, she cried and I tried to make up by promising to take her out every night the next week. We wound up having a terrible evening."

Sigmund reflected on what John had said, then proceeded with his interview, "John, if I understand you correctly, you said that when your girlfriend cries, you either try to get away from her crying ... or, at least you try not to see it. Is that right?"

John nodded, "Uhuh."

"You also said you try to cheer her up by saying nice things to her. Is that right?"

"Yes!" John spoke emphatically, leaning forward in his seat. "I hate it when she cries."

Did you notice how his girlfriend's crying controls John and restricts his behavior? Did you notice that every time his girlfriend cries John believes he has to do something about it or somehow change it? Either has to make an effort to try to get away from her crying, or he feels compelled to change it. Unfortunately, while John is trying to stop his girlfriend's crying, or trying to get away from it, he can't do other things. However, that's not the only problem. I'll bet John is careful not to do anything that might make his girlfriend cry in the first place.

Another way of looking at this situation is that his girlfriend can control John. She knows how to press his "hot buttons." By crying, or indicating that she might cry, John's girlfriend can stop him from doing certain things. This reaction has quite an effect on John's behavior. In this regard, John is not unusual. In fact, he is quite typical. Everything others say, do, or even how they look, affects almost all of us in some way.

Crying, however, doesn't **control** everyone. Other actions, such as criticism or anger, may affect us. While there may be an unlimited number of ways people can act, research shows that only a small number of actions in others over-control or restricts us.

10

At this point, let me digress for a moment, "The beginning of wisdom," said Chinese philosopher Confucius over 2500 years ago "is to call things by their correct names." Learning to use the language of *Pressing Your Own Buttons*™ is one of the first important steps of your road to freedom. By the end of the book, you—not others—will be in control of your life.

Since using the correct language is so important, from now on I'll call what others say, do, or how they look, "social stimuli."[5]

That other people's behavior, their social stimuli, affects us may come as no surprise to you. We have all experienced this phenomenon. However, as with John, some things people say, do, or even how they look can affect us too much. They can affect us so much that we no longer act freely in their presence. I think you'll agree that when his girlfriend started to cry, or even looked like she might cry, John didn't feel free to do what he wanted to do.

Take a minute or two now to think of some social stimulus you can't stand. For example, I used to find a student ignoring me quite frustrating. You may find another stimulus affects you. You might want to jot some of these down now to refer to later.

Did you make your list? Good. Now, let's go back to John's situation. It's reasonable to guess that John would be freer to respond more rationally if he got used to his girlfriend's crying and he could think of more and better ways to deal with her tears. Wouldn't you agree?

In fact, all of us becoming freer with our behavior is a very worthwhile goal. That is one of the benefits of *Pressing Your Own Buttons*™; you'll have more freedom in your own behavior.

At this point, let me assure you that in mastering the strategies in *Pressing Your Own Buttons*™, there is no danger that you'll become a cold, mean, nasty, or otherwise horrid individual. Just the opposite will happen. By the time you've completed this book, I am confident you will have become a kinder, more compassionate person.

One of the main goals of this learning system, is to help you identify other people's behavior—their social stimuli—which interfere with you acting freely and effectively around them. In short, you'll learn to manage you before others do.

We'll begin by helping you change your feelings about other people's reactions or social stimuli. I'll help you change your evaluations of those reactions, and teach you how to reinterpret those social stimuli. When you change your feelings about reactions such as crying, anger, ignoring, commanding, or being affectionate, you will be freer and more able to deal with others.

This book shows you techniques for reinterpreting, and getting used to, social stimuli that bother you now. I'll explain the various strategies and techniques as we go along.

Before going on to the next chapter, write down any questions you have about what I have said so far. Jot down any concerns you may have as well. Doing so will help you focus on different parts of the process that you'll learn as we go along. I assure you, as we work together through *Pressing Your Own Buttons*™ I will address all your questions and concerns. For now, before we go on to the next chapter, take time to jot them down. Do so while they are still fresh in your mind. As we go along, I will answer them. That way you'll get the maximum benefit from the book.

Chapter Summary

No one is an island. You and I, indeed all humans, need to interact with other people. Who and what we are at any given point in our lives, is a result of what we learn, directly or indirectly, from other people. That is because our brains are like digital recorders. Every one of our life experiences passes through our brains. Some of those experiences stay in our short-term memories for, well, a short time. Others, our brains record and they stay there for our lifetimes. Some of those experiences are positive and helpful; they can even be life saving. Other experiences are negative. Over time, they may prove to be unhelpful even damaging.

The significant people in our lives affect us considerably, often for good, but not always so. By what they say, do, and by how they look they make impressions on the digital recorders that are our brains. It's as if the behavior of others presses our "Record" **REC** buttons and what they say, do, and how they look gets stored in our heads. Later, similar people that remind us of what we heard and saw our significant others do, say, or even look like, press our "Play" ▶ buttons and we play back these recordings. If the experiences recorded earlier are positive, we continue to play the recording.

At other times, however, the recordings that we play back are negative. The people that remind us of them seem to press our "Stop" ■ buttons. They make us hesitant and cautious and may even make us so *tense* we seem unable to function at all in their presence. There are also times when the behavior of other people presses our "Rewind" ◀◀ or "Fast Forward" ▶▶ buttons. We want to *avoid* altogether the memories and feelings these people generate in us.

In each of these situations, we are reacting impulsively, and automatically, even irrationally to the messages already recorded in our brains. We are responding to those things that our significant others—parents, friends, bosses, teachers, siblings, among others—did or said, or to how they looked that at some time earlier affected us so powerfully that it "recorded" itself on our brains at the time, and we may not now even be conscious of it.

Sound familiar? Of course it does. Like the rest of us, you have had experiences like that. Think how much better you would feel if you could take control and make a reasoned and rational response. Then you, not they, would be pressing your buttons—the buttons you choose. You could rationally choose to rewind the old recording, press your "Record" button, and lay down a whole new track by recording new thoughts over the old memories. You would then be able to *"Take control of your life so others don't!"*™

You see, whenever we impulsively and irrationally *tense* in the presence of, *avoid*, or try to *change* the troubling behavior of others—specifically those whose behavior can be quite troubling at times—we put them in control. In effect, we give them permission to press our buttons! We put them in control of us. We allow them to press our "hot buttons."[6] As long as the speech, actions, and/or appearance of others control our behavior, we are no longer free to be the people we could be.

The more familiar you are with the total program, the more proficient you will become. Before long, I believe you will understand the program as well as I.

Although the later Chapters build on the concepts and skills taught in earlier ones, some material does overlap and is repeated from chapter to chapter. This repetition is intentional and will help fix the concepts in your mind as you master them.

From time to time, as you read the material in the various lessons, I will ask you to complete some brief **activities**. These are **very important!** They reinforce the concepts you will be learning and give you some direct experience with the important ideas trained in the ***Pressing Your Own Buttons***™ learning system. These ideas and concepts will enable you to act more freely at home or at work, in fact anywhere you might find yourself in the company of others.

Think of these activities, as miniature experiments in which you can try out the techniques you'll be learning. Doing these activities, as and when asked to do so, will help you discover for yourself many effective and ineffective ways of behaving. Each exercise is the result of much careful research and is an integral part of ***Pressing Your Own Buttons***™. That you have a clear and detailed understanding of what you are to do *before* you do any of the exercises is essential. Therefore, read the instructions carefully. They will explain the activities to you. Then, and only then, carry out the assignments. Be sure to do each of them in turn. They'll help to ensure your success.

Chapter 2:

"Hot Buttons"-Troublesome Social Stimuli

Margaret dreaded going to her parents' for the holidays. Doing so was always a hassle. "You never visit me," Mother always complained. "I never get to see you anymore." Yet, although they lived a country apart, Margaret did visit her mother 2-3 times a year.

Then there was Dad. He continually argued with Mom, who never seemed to quit nagging him. Margaret got sick to her stomach just thinking about going home for the holiday. "Oh, God, I wish I could just stay home," she thought as the conflict between going and staying raged insider her. And, the problem didn't stop there. Margaret would also get angry with herself, as she felt so guilty for not being "a caring daughter."

For Margaret, going home was a no-win situation. On the other hand, when she and husband Mark went to be with his family on the alternate holidays it was a very different story. Margaret looked forward to going. They always had fun there.

"Oh, it's so good to have you!" Mark's mother would declare as Margaret and he walked in the door. There were no complaints about how seldom they got together. Quite the opposite, the Porters were very grateful for the time they could spend together—especially with the grandchildren. There were never any recriminations and that sick feeling Margaret always got in the pit of her stomach as she turned her thoughts towards her parents' home, never materialized. In fact, leaving to return home was difficult.

Clearly, her mother's criticizing her troubles—even controls—Margaret. She gets tense, wants to avoid even talking with her mom. What is more, Margaret gets angry with herself for feeling the way she does. Interestingly, when his mother criticizes Mark in some way, Margaret isn't troubled at all.

The fact that the same stimulus — anger, hostility, criticism, disapproval, ignoring, unresponsiveness, affection, friendliness, commanding, issuing orders, being firm, or sadness, crying, impulsivity (and perhaps even smell and taste)[7]— can affect us differently coming from different people is quite common. That's because all social stimuli (what people say, do, or how they look) are concrete and very specific. Keeping in mind that a social stimulus is anything a person does, says, or even how the person looks, then everyone must generate a great many social stimuli. We all laugh, cry, shout, frown, and smile. We can all be friendly, stern, attack others, or make unkind remarks. All these behaviors —and a whole lot more that people generate—are also social stimuli. The ones we like are like green lights to us. Those we don't like are "rewind" and "fast forward" buttons that make us want to *avoid* them, or like "rewind" and "re-record" buttons, that tell us we should *change* them instead. Sometimes, they cause us to get very uncomfortable when we encounter them. Then, they act like "stop" buttons, and make us *tense*!

However, just as Mark's mother criticizing him affects Margaret in a different way than her own mother criticizing her, one person crying is quite different from the same person laughing, or scowling. Moreover, although laughing, scowling, and crying are all social stimuli, each can have a different effect on us.

The reason for this is quite simple. As I said earlier, social stimuli are both specific and concrete. For example, Margaret's mother

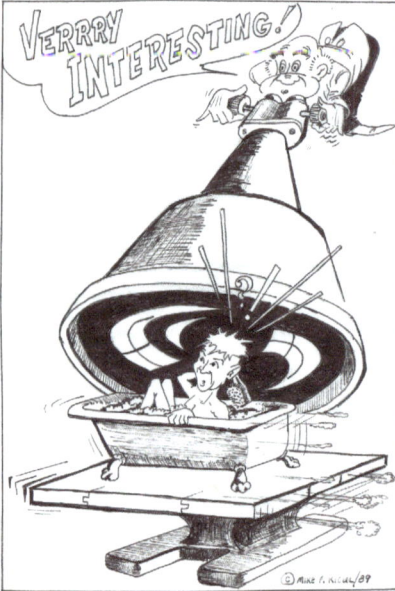

being critical ("stop" button presser for Margaret) is distinctly different from her mother laughing (a "play" button presser). Her father's being angry with her mother (another "stop" button presser) is very different from his being angry with someone else, even Margaret (an "pause" button presser at best). What is more, his mother being critical of Mark is a distinctly different social stimulus than her mother being critical of Margaret.

In addition, when Margaret's father shouts, Margaret reacts quite differently than when Mark shouts at her—or when he shouts at a football game (a definite "play" button presser)!

At this point, let's take some time to look at social stimuli in more detail. When we talk about a **stimulus**, we are talking about a *physical* property of an object. Such properties as texture, sound, color, smell, flavor, and so forth are all **stimuli**.

Social stimuli are just like these, except social stimuli refer to people. That is to say, a social stimulus is any thing a <u>person</u> says, does, or even how he or she looks. Social stimuli are what you notice when a person shouts, gives orders, looks helpless, or remains quiet. When we talk about social stimuli, then, we are always talking about the physical, observable properties of a person. Only social stimuli, then, can refer to what a person actually does, says, or how a person actually looks. They are always observable and never depend on what we think. Consequently, when a person frowns, we *can* say, "She's frowning." However, we *cannot* conclude she is sad. Isn't it quite possible that a person frowning could be in deep thought? They could even have a headache. Wouldn't you agree?

When we say, "He looks sad," we are not describing a social stimulus. Sadness is *not* a social stimulus. Rather it is an **interpretation** or **inference** about what a social stimulus—like frowning, or crying—might mean. Remember, a social stimulus is always specific and concrete. Social stimuli are always observable and we must be careful how we interpret them. An incorrect interpretation or inference could lead to a response that causes

more harm than good. It might even make a bad situation worse.

To summarize, **social stimuli** are simply the actions, speech, and appearance of people. **Only people are sources of social stimuli**.

We can all smile, laugh, cry, shout, and stamp our feet. We can also turn away, get a tight feeling in our stomachs, avoid others, and so forth. Therefore, to conclude that we can all produce an almost unlimited number of different social stimuli seems quite logical. However, while the potential is there, most of us don't produce very many social stimuli. In fact, we can most

19

successfully focus our attention on just a few different kinds of stimuli.

People may act friendly and smile. They may say pleasant things to us. Others may frown or cry. Sometimes people don't seem to respond at all. They seem to ignore us altogether. Still others may act in a verbally offensive way. They may even attack us physically.

Sometimes people look hurt or disappointed. On the other hand, they may appear bright and joyful—smiling, laughing and giggling like children. They can also appear overly emotional and irrational. They could lose control of themselves altogether: crying, screaming, and shouting, calling us names, or even ranting and raving.

Still others are commanding. Even when they aren't in charge, they give orders to anyone and everyone.

You can think of other kinds of stimuli. The ones I've just mentioned include most of what people usually do, say, or how they look.

Try this. Take a few minutes right now. Think about people you have known. Recall their behavior in as much detail as you can. Get vivid pictures of them behaving in any of the five ways I mentioned earlier.

Write down some of your recollections as you try to imagine what these people said, did, or how they looked. Consider a variety of situations in which they behaved as you picture them. Writing down what you recall, will prove very helpful later in the book. As you make your notes, be as specific as possible. Make note only of what the people <u>actually</u> said, <u>actually </u> did, or how they actually looked. Be very specific.

Take care to avoid interpreting what you think their behavior meant. What they <u>actually</u> do, say, or how they look is very important. We'll deal later with what these behaviors may mean to you.

For example, make notes like:

> "My father was shouting, and his teeth were clenched. I could see his hand make a fist. Then, he pounded the desk. "I don't have to put up with this crap!" he shouted. "No one is going to tell me how to do my job!""

Notice I identified the person. Then, I wrote exactly what I recalled "Father" saying, doing, and how he looked. I didn't say he was angry. Instead, I noted exactly what I saw and heard. To say, "My father was angry," is to put a label on his behavior. That label may not accurately describe what Father said, did, or even how he looked. Simply saying, "My father was angry," doesn't give a clear enough picture. When some people describe others as angry, the "others" may not shout, pound their fists, curse, or clench their teeth at all. They may only say negative things.

Unfortunately, simply saying someone is "angry" doesn't give the whole picture. Another individual may interpret what appears to be anger quite differently. In fact, the person observed may not be angry at all. What if, for example, you found out that individual was just rehearsing a part in an upcoming play at the community theatre! How embarrassing if you reacted as if they were angry with you!

21

While I did not intend for you to take this last alternative seriously, nevertheless you can see how important it is to be very specific about what you actually see, hear, and feel. Just as in my examples, the social stimuli you see and describe must always be concrete and specific.

Just as different people emit different social stimuli, the effect their stimuli have on you is different too. For example, your mother getting angry is different from your father getting angry. Your boss getting angry will be different again. What is more, your father, mother, or boss giving you an order is quite different from their laughing or their ignoring you.

I've been an educator for more than forty years, and I can tell you that a student being critical of me is different from a colleague or my principal being critical. My wife being critical is different again. How a social stimulus affects us, therefore, depends on the particular stimulus and on the person that generates it. I'll explain more in the next chapter.

Chapter 3:

Observation, Inference, and Evaluation

This chapter is particularly important. Here, I'll show you how to look differently at the things people say, do, and how they look. This is the first step in learning to identify them and then to change your reactions to them. By the end of the Pressing Your Own Buttons, you'll be freer to function the way you really want to function. Imagine driving your car and at every intersection, you have a green light!

Changing either your evaluations of your troublesome social stimuli, or how you react to them, is the key to stopping people from pressing your personal hot buttons.

Consider this. What really happens when you look at or listen to someone? Simply put, you see or hear something. That's obvious, isn't it?

Isn't it also true that after looking at or after listening to other people you react in some way? For example, depending upon what they say or do, you might talk back, frown, move away,

cry, or hug them. You might even want to hit them! Although I don't recommend you do.

In fact, you could do many things in response to their words or actions. You could even react to the appearance of the other person, couldn't you?

This, too, is obvious. Be aware though, observing and reacting aren't all that happens. When we look at people, or listen to them, at least four different things occur. Most of us are not even aware of them all. First, we observe them. We look at people, and we listen to them. Then we react. We do something in response to what they say, do, or to how they look. That seems simple enough doesn't it?

However, between the time we observe and the time we respond, two other important things happen that are not so obvious at all. Once we observe a social stimulus, we then make an *inference* about it. Next, we *evaluate* what we observe. We might even evaluate our inference about what we have just observed. Only after we observe a social stimulus, make an inference about it, and then evaluate the stimulus or inference, do we then react.

Let's consider an example that will help clarify the distinction among **observation**, **inference**, and *evaluation*. Four-year-old Cathy was a birthday girl. Watching her daughter eyeing the candle-covered birthday cake, Mother noticed a frown on Cathy's face. Mother could see the child holding her stomach. Cathy's much-loved Teddy dangled from her limp hand. Many interpretations of these observations ran through Mother's mind. All of them were wrong! Cathy had just eaten too many candies earlier and wasn't feeling up to cake at this point despite the joyful occasion.

Sometimes describing in words what we see and hear is difficult. Fortunately, how accurately we can describe what we observe is not too important. What's important is that our observations give us a clear picture, or clear mental image, of what we see or hear. Just as in our own situations, John not only observed the social stimulus of his girlfriend being sad or crying, he also made *inferences* about it. Like us, John also went the next step and *evaluated* what he observed. He inferred his girlfriend was sad and unhappy, and evaluated that as bad.

We all evaluate our inferences. However, we don't all infer the same things, or evaluate the same stimulus, in the same way. For example, two people observing the same person crying might evaluate the crying differently. One might consider crying an ordinary activity that doesn't hurt anyone. The other observer might consider the crying dreadful or even painful.

In summary: evaluation is concerned with whether we consider something good or bad, and with whether it is necessary to change it or not. Usually—and often automatically—we'll think about changing what we consider bad. On the other hand, we will usually try to maintain a stimulus we evaluate as good.

You must be very clear on this; evaluation is different from observation, or inference. Often, how we evaluate a stimulus is arbitrary. We base our evaluations on our own notions or ideas of what is good or bad, and not always on any principle or rule. Evaluations, therefore, are often arbitrary. Our current evaluations of social stimuli depend on the kinds of experiences we've had with others as we grew up. Some individuals growing up in a particular family may have learned that a sad look is bad. They might feel that they have to do something about it.

On the other hand, another individual, in a different family, might have learned that sadness is not so bad at all and we should allow people to experience it. We have all learned many evaluations from our parents and others. Moreover, as I have said before, we not only evaluate social stimuli themselves, but we also evaluate the inferences we make about those stimuli.

Unfortunately, the inferences we make could be wrong or inaccurate.

For example, we might observe someone frowning and infer from the frowning that the person is angry when, in fact, the individual is merely deep in thought. We might then mistakenly evaluate our inference of "anger" as a bad thing and feel compelled to do something about the other person's anger.

If the individual was deep in thought and was not angry, then the very act of doing something about it will have created a problem. You can see, then, that our evaluations are important in determining how we will act or respond to other people.

26

At this point, it is important to understand that our evaluations always depend on what experiences we have had with others. Our evaluations depend on what we have learned either from interacting with others or from observing, others interact. You'll learn more about this later. For now, though, I must point out that we can change our feelings and behavior by changing our evaluations of social stimuli. Later, I'll show you how to change your evaluations if, and I stress "if," your evaluations are not helping you.

Here's something you can try. It will help you to get a fix on some of the inferences you make, and on some of the evaluations that relate to them. Take a few minutes now to try it. Then, when you've finished, continue with the chapter.

For any one of your Mother, Father, Boss, Teacher, or Friend, think of a time when they were (1) critical or disapproving, (2) angry or hostile, (3) sad or crying, (4) affectionate or friendly, (5) giving orders—commanding, (6) ignoring. In each case, and for each person, what did you observe?

Be very specific. For example, you might write, "I saw him clench his fist, then shake it threateningly at the boy while swearing loudly at him." Clearly, that's more precise than saying, "He was angry at the boy." Always report *exactly* what you see and hear. Avoid the temptation to interpret your observations.

What inferences did you make? What were your evaluations of those inferences? Were they bad, good, or sinful? You may want to take some extra time and do this for all three.

We usually give this activity to participants in the **Pressing Your Own Buttons**™ seminars and boot camps. Let's look in on one of these to see how Mary deals with this exercise.

Turning to Mary, Sigmund opened the next part of the session, "Thank you Mary for volunteering to share what you've

27

written. Let's start with the first social stimulus you noted. What did you write down?'"

Mary was eager to share. She wanted to understand more about how her boyfriend's anger was controlling her behavior, "I wrote down, 'My boyfriend shouting.'"

Sigmund probed deeper, "Describe him to me, please. Give me all your observations and be as specific as you can."

"Well," said Mary thoughtfully, "his voice was loud. His face was red . . . and . . . well . . . he was pointing and waving his finger at me."

"Did he say anything?"

"Yes!" Mary replied without hesitation. "He said he hated it when I was late. He accused me of being late on purpose."

"Anything else?" Sigmund continued.

"Uh . . . his breathing was heavy and he began pacing back and forth."

"That's fine, Mary." Sigmund was encouraging and supportive. "You have been very specific in what you saw, and heard. That's good! Now, tell me about your inferences. What did you write for them?"

Mary looked thoughtfully at her notes. She waited, and then replied, "I wrote that my boyfriend was really upset. I said he was really angry."

"And what about your evaluation?"

"Well," Mary continued, still referencing her notes, "it's not very good for him to get so upset. I don't like it when he gets so angry."

"Thank you Mary. How about the rest of you?" Sigmund waited for a response from the others in the group. "Do all of you agree with Mary's inference that her boyfriend was angry?" Again, he waited.

George responded with some hesitation, "Yes … I'd agree he was upset. But I don't think that's such a bad thing. It's good to get it out of your system. I mean," George paused for some time as he thought about what he might have done, "if I get all tense because I'm angry, shouting and getting it out sometimes makes me feel better. Besides, he might not really have been angry with Mary. Perhaps he was still mad at his boss for asking him to work on his day off."

Sigmund gave the group and himself some time to think over what George had said. Then, the counselor continued to question him. "So, would you say that if you saw him shouting you wouldn't necessarily think he was upset at Mary? You wouldn't evaluate it as bad. Is that right?"

"No," said George quite confidently, "I'd think it was no big deal."

You can see that George and Mary have drawn very different inferences and have made quite different evaluations about the boyfriend's shouting. Likewise, we all make similar inferences and evaluations about the behavior—the social stimuli—of others. In fact, it's common for any two people to observe the same social stimulus but make completely different inferences and evaluations about that same behavior.

Let me stress, our inferences, and evaluations are often wrong. That's when we get into trouble. When we act on such false assumptions, or make incorrect evaluations, we open the door to the behavior of others controlling us. It is then that we tend to act automatically and inappropriately. In the following chapters, I will show you how to interrupt this process so that you can act rationally and effectively. Then you'll be able to *"**Take control of your life so others don't!**"*™

Chapter 4:

Is What You Thought They Said What They Meant?

Remember what Confucius said? In Chapter 1, I told you he said, "The beginning of wisdom is to call things by their correct name." Well, who doesn't want to be wise, right? The purpose of this chapter is to help you make even wiser use of language in a concrete and specific manner. Doing so will help you be more accurate and precise in describing your button pressers—what we call **"social stimuli"**[8]—and in describing your own actions as well.

Let's begin by considering how people use language. In their work with the principles in ***Pressing Your Own Buttons***™, researchers have found that people often make inaccurate use of language. People also fail to use language concretely. This is most often true when people use abstract, general terms and labels. Research shows that we regularly misuse words such as "angry," "affectionate," "critical," "depressed," "unresponsive," "impulsive," and "commanding," among others.

All too often, people don't describe an observation or an action very well at all. Consequently, the person listening to them, and even the people themselves, may not get an accurate or clear picture of what is being talked about.

Do you remember Mary? Let's drop in on her group again and see how she sometimes makes inappropriate use of language.

> "Mary," Sigmund said softly as he turned to face her. "Earlier, you said your boyfriend was really mad at you. From your statement, it is difficult for me to understand what you mean. The problem is that different people use the word "mad" in so many different ways. Tell me again, what did your boyfriend look like? What did he say? What did he do?"
>
> Mary seemed puzzled by this. She wore a slight frown on her face, and squirmed a bit in her chair. Placing her folded hands into her lap, she replied, "Well ... he was shouting. He had a frown on his face ... and ... and ... his eyes were wide open."
>
> Sigmund paused before speaking, "Uh ... hmmm. I'm beginning to get a better idea. Can you recall any details?"
>
> "Yes," Mary said, as she became noticeably more relaxed. Her hands remained folded in her lap. "He was pointing his finger at me. He said he hated it when I was late. He even accused me of doing it on purpose because I didn't like going to the hockey games. Then he shouted and swore at me, 'I like the bloody games, even if you don't!'"
>
> The members of the group looked at each other. "Thank you, Mary," Sigmund continued, "Now, I have a much clearer picture of your boyfriend in that situation." The others nodded in agreement.

At first, Mary was not precise in her description of her boyfriend. With Sigmund's helpful questioning, she became more accurate in those descriptions. In a similar way, like Mary, we all too frequently describe other people's actions in an unclear way. We may also describe our own actions inappropriately. Let's follow along again to see how Sigmund handled this.

His attentions now focused on the entire group, Sigmund continued. "To help you all become more accurate and precise in your use of language, let's examine one possible description about ourselves. Let's take the phrase, 'I was terribly depressed when I failed the exam.'

"Have any of you ever said something like that?" Sigmund paused. Looking among the group, he fixed his gaze on Ted. "Ted, have you? … Okay then … try to paint an accurate picture for me of what you looked like and what you did, or said. Tell me what you were thinking. And, tell me about any sensations you experienced."

Ted seemed surprised at first. After a few moments of reflection he collected himself and replied, "Yeah … I remember a time when I was depressed because my father was crying. I got tense all over. I felt like leaving the room. He just got off the phone. My uncle called to say that my grandfather had died. I'd never seen my dad cry before.

"My throat got really tight, I wanted to say something, but I froze. I remember thinking, 'I wish he'd stop crying.' My stomach tensed up and I felt helpless. My face showed it! Eventually, I did leave the room and started to cry, too. I really loved my grandfather."

"Thanks, Ted," Sigmund spoke more softly than before. "That seems like it was a very difficult time for you." He inferred this from Ted's sad look and trembling lip. "Now, I think I understand much better what you mean by 'depressed.'"

At this point, you should have a better idea of why you need to use language that is both **specific** and **concrete**. Words such as "mad" and "depressed" need clarification because they often mean different things to different people. In fact, you might not have considered Ted "depressed" at all. Always be specific and use concrete words. Consider the following.

If I said to you, "My boss seemed really angry when I got into work yesterday." What would that mean to you? What picture of the boss comes into mind? What do you imagine her saying to me? How might she be saying it? With what tone of voice? Is she loud? What does her face look like? How is she standing? For instance, has she folded her arms? Was she even angry with me at all, or was someone, or something else, the cause? You might even consider whether she was even angry at all. For instance, do you hear her using angry words, shouting, or just standing quietly?

From this example, you can see there are many possible inferences and evaluations we could make. While they could be correct, they just as easily could be wrong!

I once had a friend who always looked like he was mad at the world. He seldom smiled. Yet, he was usually jovial, fun to be with, and had a very keen wit. Not at all was he, as he appeared to be to most people who observed him. Only when one had gotten to know him did the first impression change.

Before going on to the next chapter, I'd like you to experiment a bit more. I want you to ask a friend or another member of your family to do the same exercise. Pay careful attention to their observations, inferences, and evaluations. How are they like yours? How are they different?

Once you've compared your observations with theirs, you'll have an even better understanding of the importance of language. You'll be more aware of how important it is to be specific and concrete in your observations and in your use of words.

Now you are ready to identify some of your own controlling or interfering social stimuli.

Chapter 5:

Your Personal "Hot Buttons"

This chapter will help you identify specific social stimuli—the button pressers—that may be controlling or interfering with you.

Remember what you learned earlier. Everyone is a source of social stimuli. Everyone is a potential button presser. Yes, even you and I might press other people's buttons. What we say, what we do, and how we look, affect others. The reverse is also true. Everything others say to us, what they do, and even how they look, affects us.

Some social stimuli make us smile, shout for joy, even want to hug someone. On the other hand, some social stimuli make us tense up.

Or, we may feel like avoiding them. We might even try to change them. Those social stimuli we avoid, change, or which make us tense up, we call **controlling** or **interfering** social stimuli.

You have already spent time observing social stimuli and noting how they affect you. You saw that crying, criticizing, hostile actions, ordering, and so forth, could affect you markedly. In this chapter, I'll show you how to identify the specific social stimuli that interfere with your acting freely. By the time you finish **Chapter 5**, you'll have a small list of social stimuli that affect you. Specifically, we will look for the kinds of social stimuli that you try to avoid, try to change, or that lead you to tense up in some way. They're also the kinds of stimuli that you expect so you are careful not to do anything that will make them occur.

First, take five minutes to recall three situations in which you remember feeling uncomfortable. Picture how you reacted in those situations. What did the other people say? What did they do? What did they look like? What did you say? What did you do? What were you thinking? Did you want to get away? Did you want to change things? Did you feel tense?

Think hard about each situation. Take time to jot down some ideas about all three. When you are finished, continue with your reading.

Finished? Excellent! Look at what you've recalled. Chances are you made note of several social stimuli. Perhaps, someone frowned. Someone else might have shouted or made some negative remarks. Yet, another person could have been quiet and said nothing at all.

What about you, did you feel like changing anything? Did you feel like getting away? Perhaps you might now feel like avoiding a situation where any one or more of these behaviors might happen again. Consider also whether you tensed up.

If you thought or felt any of these things, then at least one social stimulus you recalled stops you from acting freely. You'll recall that any social stimulus that interferes with

36

your acting freely is a controlling or interfering social stimulus.

Take some time to consider further, what you recalled. Which, social stimuli, had an interfering effect on you. Which are your button pressers? To help you do this we have prepared a special form for you. You'll find it in **Appendix A**. Now, look at the form. Notice, that in the left-hand column, there are listed five important people in your life: "Mother," "Father," "Teacher," "Boss," and "Close Friend." Below each important person we have listed five kinds of reactions that person might have shown. We label these reactions "Critical," "Anger," "Sadness," and "Friendly," "Commanding," and "Ignoring."[9]

Across the top of the form, there are three columns labeled, "(1) Others' Behavior and Appearance," "(2) My Reactions," and "(3) Type of Reaction."

Let me explain how to use the form. Consider the first stimulus listed, "Mother," being critical. Think of a specific time when your mother criticized you or disapproved of you. Recall the situation in as much detail as possible. Recall what led up to her criticizing or disapproving. Get a vivid picture or image of what her face looked like. What *exactly* did she say? Be as specific and concrete as possible. Try to remember how she said it. Make note of details such as her hand or any other movements.

With a vivid picture in your mind of the situation, in Column (1) write down a brief description such as "talking loudly, staring at me, tense face, shaking finger at me," and so forth. When you've finished, continue reading the chapter.

Finished? Good! Were your observations specific and concrete? Excellent! Now that you have completed Column (1) in as much detail as possible, look at Column (2). Recall, again in as much detail as possible, what you did or how you reacted to your mother. Did you say something to her? Did you shout back at her? Did you become quiet? Precisely what did you think? Did your muscles become tense? Try to re-live the experience and write down in

37

Column (2) a brief description of how you reacted, or what you did. Ignore the column labeled "Reactions," for the time being.

Have you completed Columns (1) and (2)? Please, do not continue unless you do so. Doing this now is very important to your progress over the next chapters.

When you wrote down your observations, you may have found yourself becoming somewhat uneasy, a little tense, or even agitated. Don't be surprised. This is quite normal. Keep in mind you're looking at social stimuli that may bother you!

Now, go back and look over your reactions to each of the social stimuli. Check to see if you did anything to avoid the stimuli. If you did, write "Avoid" in Column (3).

Take a few moments now and check your responses to the exercise to see if you did anything to change the stimuli. As before, if you did, write down "Change" in Column (3). If you became tense, write down "Tense" in Column (3). Be sure to write down the type of reaction for every stimulus you listed.

At this point, I want you to summarize what you've observed. Take another moment or two to write down all the social stimuli that you indicated earlier you try to avoid, change or which make you tense. Again, take the time now. Doing so is very important. You'll need to refer to this information in later chapters.

You now have a list of some of your button pressers, the social stimuli that you try to avoid, change, or that make you become tense. Hang on to this list. During the next week make a point of observing others and then re-check to see if you do try to avoid or change these social stimuli, or become tense in their presence. Check also to see if even anticipating these social stimuli causes you to want to change or avoid them, or to become tense in their presence.

Later we will review all of this. Then I'll help you come to some decision regarding the social stimuli that affect you. I'll also help you to identify the social stimuli that you should work on so that you can act more freely around other people.

Showing you how you learned the controlling or interfering social stimuli in the first place will be the goal of the next chapter. There we will look at some of your earlier experiences to determine how you learned to react to these social stimuli the way you do.

Chapter 6:

Where Did THAT Come From?

How did you learn to let the social stimuli you listed in the previous chapter, control you? How did they come to interfere with your acting freely? In this chapter, I'll help you find out where, when, and how this all came about.

You'll recall that social stimuli—button pressers—affect everyone. There are no exceptions to this. However, we all react differently to the things other people say, do, and even to how they look. What may be attractive, for example, in one culture may be a turn off in another. What may be quite acceptable conduct in one community could lead to isolation—even death—if done among a different group of people.

For example "thumbs up" in our culture could be a sign of a great movie—one well worth seeing—or, of having done a job well. In another country, "thumbs up" might prove to be an insult. How we learn to react to social stimuli, and how we learn to evaluate both the stimuli themselves and our own reactions to them, is quite interesting.

We'll look at this in more detail as we go along, but first let's review some of the observations you've made since **Chapter 5**. Take some time right now to look back at the lists you made earlier. Since making your observations, and recording them, have you made any changes? If you did, make note of those changes. Write them down and keep them with your earlier notes.

Did you write them down? If not, please do so now. As before, these notes will come in handy later in the book.

By now, you should have a list of some social stimuli that affect your reactions to what people look like, say, or do. Recheck your list before going on. Is it complete and accurate? If so, then you're ready to proceed.

Earlier I said your controlling or interfering social stimuli—also called troublesome social stimuli—were stimuli that made you feel you must change them, get away from them, or which made you tense up in their presence. These are your button pressers. Even when you only anticipate being in the presence of these social stimuli, they cause you to tense up, want to change, or avoid them altogether. Next, we'll consider how you might have learned that certain social stimuli are bad and, therefore, they make you react to them as you do.

We'll begin by revisiting the Pressing Your Own Buttons™ group. Joan has just told them about her experience with her mother apparently giving in to Joan's little brother.

> The tension in Joan's voice was noticeable as she shared her story. "I told my mother that I didn't think she should spoil my little brother so much."
>
> Sigmund encouraged Joan to elaborate, "How did she react to this?"

41

"She got really upset!" Joan was quite emphatic about her inference regarding what she had observed.

Sigmund probed further, "Joan, try to be more specific and concrete. What did your mother look like? What specifically did she say? What exactly did she do?"

"My Mother's face got really red. She said she didn't want to discuss it and she left the room."

"Good. That gives me a clearer picture. Can you recall how your father reacted when you criticized your mother?"

Joan tensed. Her face showed a slight frown and she got somewhat red in the face. "He was angry at me and told me that it wasn't right for me to tell my mother what to do. Actually, he called me a "smart ass" and said he didn't like me talking to her like that."

"That's helpful, Joan. You're being more specific and concrete in your words. Now, think of a time when your father criticized your mother and tell us your mother's reaction."

Joan pondered this for a while. Then she answered, in a voice more tense than before. "Any time my father criticizes my mother she becomes very quiet. Usually, she leaves and goes into her bedroom or workroom."

"From your descriptions," Sigmund summed up, "it seems that your mother tries to get away from situations involving criticism. Now, can you recall an incident when one of your brothers or sisters criticized your mother? Tell us how your mother reacted and how your father reacted."

Again, Joan waited before answering. She shifted in her seat and leaned back into the chair. "Well, one time my little brother told my mom he didn't like her new perm. My mom got all red and flustered and my dad got angry with my brother for upsetting her. He said, 'That's rude,' and made my brother apologize to my mom. After he did, my mom went upstairs to her sewing room."

"That's very specific and concrete. Thank you." Sigmund's remarks were encouraging and Joan became noticeably more relaxed. "From your descriptions I can see that in your family you had a number of experiences from which you learned that criticism is an awful thing. Your father told you and your brother directly, that criticism was bad, and by observing your mother's and your father's behavior, it would be easy for you to conclude that criticism was upsetting and must be avoided."

The situation with Joan is a good example of how we learn to evaluate a social stimulus as bad. Anytime we learn a response by watching how someone else responds in the same situation, we are learning indirectly.

Learning to respond in a particular way to a particular social stimulus, because someone tells us to respond that way, we call **direct learning.** We might also learn because significant others punish us for acting that particular way.

Now try this. Look at the chart in **Appendix B**. In the left-hand column is a list of your potential troublesome social stimuli. In the middle column, for each stimulus, write about a direct experience you have had with that stimulus. Then, in the last column, record your reaction to that direct experience, how you reacted to that stimulus. Only when you have finished doing this little exercise, go on to the next chapter.

Chapter 7:

Cooling Your "Hot Buttons"

Now, I'm going to show you how to cool your "hot buttons." I'll not only show you how to look at them differently, I'll also show you how to change your reactions to them. Changing either your evaluations of your troublesome social stimuli, or how you react to them, is the key to stopping people from pressing your personal hot buttons. By the time you're finished this section, you'll have discovered for yourself what works best for you. I'll even show you some little experiments you can do to make this whole process easier.

There are three ways of changing your reactions to troublesome social stimuli:

1. Cognitive Reappraisal.

2. Desensitization.

3. Behavior variation.

Don't be intimidated by these new words. You'll soon understand them just as well as I do.

The first is **cognitive reappraisal**. I'll simply call it **reappraisal**. Reappraisal involves looking at your troublesome social stimuli in an objective and logical way. You'll be like a scientist looking through a microscope, describing exactly what is actually there, not what she thinks is there. For example, if someone crying bothers you, think about whether his or her crying is really so terrible. Consider whether a person crying is actually hurting or suffering. Wouldn't you agree that sometimes people have tears in their eyes from laughing, or when deeply touched by some beautiful experience?

Even if they're sad, see if they get over it. Do they recover in a reasonable length of time? What *really* happens when someone cries? Rationally and objectively, thinking through the short-term and the long-term consequences of what you and others do is quite helpful. Often, the consequences of our behavior are not so bad or terrible at all. Sometimes they're even funny.

The second way of changing your reactions to troublesome social stimuli we refer to as **desensitization**. This involves focusing your attention on a troublesome social stimulus long enough for you to become less sensitive to it. Over many years of working with these ideas, we have found that if a person looks at, or listens to, a troublesome social stimulus five hundred or more times, that stimulus becomes ordinary. It no longer bothers them.

The same can happen for you even if your troublesome social stimulus is very unpleasant for you. Begin by imagining that stimulus. Do this for only a few seconds at first. Then stop. Gradually, increase the length of time that you imagine the stimulus. Soon you'll be able to imagine it clearly with little or no discomfort at all.

At first, when you imagine a troublesome social stimulus, you may have all sorts of feelings. You may even squirm a bit. Don't let that worry you. Be patient. This is normal. Just go ahead and have the feelings. Let them be. If necessary, squirm as long as you can keep a clear picture of the stimulus. In my *Pressing Your Own Buttons*™ groups, I have participants imagine a stimulus. At home, you can observe the stimulus first hand. The way to do that is to be alert to the stimulus whenever it occurs. When it does crop up, look at it, or listen to it without doing anything for just five seconds. Then do whatever comes naturally.

Whenever you observe your troublesome social stimulus, whether in your imagination or for real, it is important that you inhibit—hold back—any attempt to change the stimulus. Let me repeat that. Whenever you observe your troublesome social stimulus, whether in your imagination or for real, it is important that you hold back any attempt to change it.

At this point, if you are at all confused about **reappraisal** or **desensitization**, take the time to go back over what you've just read. When you're clear about what I mean by the terms **reappraisal** or **desensitization,** move on, but only when you are clear and there is no confusion.

The third way of changing your reactions to troublesome social stimuli is **behavior variation**. All this means is, you choose to act differently when exposed to your troublesome social stimulus. For example, suppose you usually become quiet or feel like leaving the room when someone frowns. Instead, do something different. Try walking up to the frowning person and saying something pleasant. "Hi! That's a sharp tie you have on." Okay, so they may not have on a sharp tie. You do get the idea, I trust.

Similarly, if criticism bothers you a lot, try thanking the person who criticizes you: "Thanks. I've never thought of it that way. Now I'll be able to do it better the next time." Just be sure to avoid being sarcastic. Thank them in a sincere tone of voice.

47

You can do these things either in your imagination, through imaging, or in the real situation. I'll tell you more about this later. In addition, I'll tell you how to design little experiments that will help you to vary your behavior deliberately in the presence of your troublesome stimuli.

For now, let's go back to the Pressing Your Own Buttons™ group, where Sigmund demonstrates what I've just been talking about.

> "Would someone volunteer to try reappraisal and desensitization with me?" Sigmund asked with enthusiastic anticipation. He waited for a response.
>
> Renatta hesitated, and then took the leap, "I will."
>
> "Thanks. Renatta, I want you to think of a specific time when your boyfriend cried. Can you do that?"
>
> Renatta gave it some thought, and then spoke hesitantly, "Uh … yeah."
>
> "Okay." Sigmund didn't wait. He jumped right in. "Renatta, think of that situation. Get a clear picture or image of your boyfriend crying. Notice his eyes. Are tears running down his cheeks? How does his face look? What kind of noise is he making?
>
> "Get a vivid picture of all those things. Are you able to clearly see your boyfriend crying?"
>
> Sigmund waited.
>
> After considering the situation, Renatta answered reflecting on her mind picture. "Yes … that's not too hard."
>
> "Good! Does it bother you even a little bit to picture your boyfriend in this situation?"

Again, she paused to gather her thoughts. Then, keeping the image clearly in mind, continued. "Yeah ... a little." However, after further reflection, Renatta added, "Well ... actually ... quite a bit, really!"

After a pause, Sigmund continued, "That's all right. Now, to start, I want you to imagine him crying ... but imagine it for just a few seconds. Get a clear image of his face. Picture his tears. Hear the sounds he is making.

"Now, just keep looking at those things. " After waiting for her to respond, he continued, "That's fine, Renatta. "

"Okay, you can stop. Were you able to get a clearer image this time?"

"Yes ... I can picture him clearly," she responded excitedly as if she had made a new discovery.

"Excellent! Now, as you picture him crying, try to do it as a scientist might observe him during an experiment. Get a clear mental picture of him. If it helps, pretend you're an anthropologist. Do what an anthropologist might do in real life. Think of this as interesting behavior ... something that should be studied."

She focused all her thoughts on creating a vivid, lifelike picture in her mind as Renatta sat quietly, intent on following Sigmund's instructions.

"Okay. Stop!"

The counselor's voice startled Renatta.

"Now, I want you to imagine that your boyfriend is a small child in a crib. Can you do that?" he chuckled.

"By the smile on your face, I see that you can. This time, Renatta, I want you to get a very clear picture of your boyfriend crying. Imagine he is jumping up and down in the crib."

"Just focus on that for a few seconds." Renatta complied thoughtfully.

"Now, stop again. Renatta, you could have also tried looking at your boyfriend in many other ways, couldn't you? For example, you could imagine him as a painting on a wall—like a tearful male Mona Lisa—or a crying statue of David and so forth."

"Okay ... Let's try another approach. This time, Renatta, when you imagine your boyfriend crying, I also want you to picture yourself doing something different from what you usually do. Let's see ... can you ... can you imagine yourself walking up to him, putting your hand on his shoulder and saying, 'I'm sorry you feel that way. I'm sure you'll get over it soon.'"

"Let's give that a try. You can do it. Be sure to get a vivid picture of your boyfriend crying again. Imagine yourself ... really feel yourself doing it ... walking up to him ... putting your arm on his shoulder and saying, 'I'm sorry you feel that way, but I'm sure you'll get over it soon.'"

"Good! Now, once more, get very clear pictures of him crying while you are walking up to him. Put your arms on his shoulder ... and tell him that you're sorry he feels that way."

At first, everyone could see Renatta's muscles tense as she followed Sigmund's directions. However, before long she began to relax.

"Excellent! Renatta, how do you feel right now? How is your boyfriend's crying affecting you?"

"Well ... I don't feel quite as uncomfortable as I usually do."

"That's good," Sigmund said encouragingly, "Very good.

"Here's a little homework assignment for you to do," he continued as Renatta's eyes accustomed themselves to the light once more. "Think of future possibilities when your boyfriend might cry. During the next week, be ready to observe him for five seconds before you do anything. Just look at him for five seconds. Then, when the five seconds are up, go ahead and act as you usually do".

"I want you to do this as often as you possibly can. If you're up to it, when he really does cry, go up to him, and put your arms on his shoulder. Try saying something like, 'I'm sorry you feel the way you do.'"

"If you don't feel up to it at this point, we can do some more focusing on the social stimulus of your boyfriend crying, right here in the group. However, you could try the same thing at home on your own. The important thing is the more you do it, the less you'll be troubled by your boyfriend's crying."

"I'm more comfortable than usual right now," Renatta confirmed.

"Great! ... Just one more thing before we stop. Let's think of your boyfriend's crying again. You've seen him crying on more than one occasion haven't you?"

Renatta responded without hesitation, "Lots of times! He's very emotional."

"Tell me ...what happens to him when he cries?"

"I'm not certain what you mean. Nothing much happens really."

"Well, for example, how long does he cry?" Sigmund probed.

"That depends." Renatta paused, "Sometimes it's over in a few minutes. Other times it takes longer. Sometimes he only has tears in his eyes ... but nothing else happens."

Sigmund continued to explore this point. "Does he lose his appetite and quit eating?"

"No." Renatta's answer was short and to the point. She didn't even have to think about it.

"Does he lose much sleep?"

"No ... I don't think so ... not that I know of anyway."

"How long does it take before he recovers and is back to normal again?"

"Not very long at all, really." Renatta smiled at this and had a slight chuckle in her voice as she considered this last question.

"In other words," Sigmund said as he concluded this part of the session, "Crying doesn't seem to hurt him at all. In fact, isn't it possible that crying may be good for him? Perhaps crying lubricates his eyes and increases his blood circulation. If we think carefully about your boyfriend crying, we see that nothing terrible or dreadful actually happens to him or anyone else as a result. Isn't that right?"

Renatta seemed surprised as she spoke, "Yeah! I suppose so ... when you put it that way."

"Renatta," Sigmund continued, "I know that you have strong feelings about your boyfriend crying. However, I'll help you change your feelings about this troublesome social stimulus. Just for interest, let's check to see where you might have learned to think that crying is a bad thing and you must change it. Looking over some of the notes you've made, you might have used your father as a model because he tended to become upset when your brother cried. Isn't that right?"

Renatta nodded in agreement.

"Perhaps, though," Sigmund continued, "it's all right for your father to be upset about your brother's crying. However, it may not be good for you to let your boyfriend crying upset you."

The counselor then turned and addressed the whole group to summarize. "That's how we go about changing our evaluations of, and our reactions to, troublesome social stimuli. There are many variations on this approach and I'm sure you can think of some novel ones, too." With that, Sigmund ended the demonstration. "Thanks Renatta for helping us out."

What you've just seen Sigmund, the group's counselor, do with Renatta is sometimes difficult to do by yourself. However, doing so will be much easier if you first consider each of the troublesome stimuli in your list. Then follow the **Seven Simple Steps to Personal Freedom**™ I am about to explain to you. As I explain them, try to recall the demonstration in the ***Pressing Your Own Buttons***™ group you just read about where Sigmund helped Renatta deal with her boyfriend's crying. Doing so, will help you better understand the process.

Before going on to the next chapter, I want to take a few moments to show you how to use the same seven steps the counselor used to begin to help desensitize Renatta to her boyfriend's crying. Later, you will see how he used the **Seven Simple Steps to Personal Freedom**™ to help Dave cope with his father's yelling. Follow each of the steps when working with your own troublesome social stimuli—the ones you put on your personal list earlier. If you have particular difficulty dealing with one or more of your troublesome social stimuli, I recommend that you contact **Pressing Your Own Buttons**™ and arrange to speak with a counselor. Alternatively, you could take part in one of our workshops or teleconferences. To get more information, or to register for one of the teleconferences or boot camps, go to our website at http://www.garyscreatonpage.com.

Okay, are you ready? Begin by looking at your list of troublesome social stimuli and the situations that bother you. Choose <u>one</u> of them for this experiment. I suggest you choose the least

troublesome stimulus or situation. The purpose of all this is to make you more familiar with the **Seven Simple Steps to Personal Freedom**™. I want you to succeed and you'll have the best chance for success at this stage if you choose your least troublesome stimulus. It's always better to start with a small win and later to work up to situations that are more difficult. You must walk before you can run.

STEP 1: Imagine the stimulus. Get a clear picture of it.

STEP 2: Pretend you are a scientist looking at this situation. You can see and hear everything. However, you're behind a two-way mirror and no one can see or hear you. What exactly do you see happening? What does the other person look like? What does the other person say? What does the other person do? What exactly do you hear? What exactly do you say? What exactly do you do, or feel like doing?

Remember: Write the *exact* words spoken. Describe *exactly* what you see, hear, and what others involved do.

STEP 3: Imagine the other person in a cage. Get this picture in your mind. For example, you might imagine yourself as a scientist examining their behavior as they do their thing.

At first, you do this for just a few seconds at a time. Over the next day or two, picture the other person for longer and longer periods.

STEP 4: Now that you're more comfortable imagining the other person in the cage, picture yourself doing something different from what you usually do. Try many different pictures in your mind.

STEP 5: When are you going to see this person again? When the above situation comes up again, do STEPS 1 through 4—for real this time!

At first, just look at the person. As this becomes easier, think of yourself doing STEP 4.

STEP 6: What really happens? What does the other person actually do? Do they get sick? Do they get over it? The stimulus isn't so bad is it? What happens to you? Do you get sick? Do you get hurt physically? Chances are the situation isn't so bad or terrible.

STEP 7: Try to find out how you learned to do what you do. What did your father do when he saw or heard this stimulus? What did he say? What did he look like? What did your mother do? What did your mother say? What did she look like?

Now you have a clearer understanding of the steps involved in dealing with troublesome social stimuli. To help you remember all seven steps I have created a summary sheet in **Appendix C**. You may wish to copy it and display it where you will see it often.

Now, let's return to our Pressing Your Own Buttons™ group. As we do, we find them part way into a new session. Let's see how Sigmund uses the Seven Simple Steps to Personal Freedom™ to help Dave cope with his father's yelling.

"Dave," Sigmund began as he leaned forward in his chair. "Let's take one stimulus that you find troublesome and see what you usually do."

"When my father yells at me about my work, it bothers me a lot. I usually start to yell back and we get into a big fight." Dave was noticeably tense. Unlike Sigmund, he sat back in his seat as if to pull away from the counselor.

Sigmund continued, "What are the alternative ways you could act when he starts to yell at you? Dave, what could you do that you may not now be doing when your father yells?"

Dave thought for a moment, then spoke hesitantly, "Well ... I guess I can leave the room ... or ... not shout back ... And, I guess I could try to discuss the problem with him more reasonably. But, that's not what I feel like doing."

"Let's look at your suggestions." Sigmund ignored the last part of Dave's statement. Instead, he focused on the alternatives Dave offered. "They seem to me to be good ones. Do you think you could try to speak in a normal voice and tell your father you would prefer to discuss the problem with him? Dave, could you say something like, 'Dad, I can see you're upset. Maybe it would help if we sat down and talked about it'?"

Dave pondered the counselor's question. "I don't know ... maybe ... Yes, I guess so."

"Okay then. Let's try it out here, right now. Let's rehearse what you might say and do the next time. For example, how might you talk or act differently than you usually do?"

Sitting forward in his seat now, and leaning toward Sigmund, Dave replied, "Well, I could sit down and say, 'Dad, I know you're upset because I'm not doing as well as you think I should. Maybe we could talk about it without yelling at each other.'"

Sigmund smiled. "That sounds good. I suggest you to write down what you'll do and say. You don't want you to forget anything. Then, during the week carry out what you've planned here. No matter how uncomfortable you feel about it, just do, and say what you said and did now. The next time your father yells at you, try the alternatives you just practiced with me.

"Dave, I want to encourage you to pay particular attention to how your father responds. Notice what he says. See what he does, and how he looks. Think of this, as an experiment to discover what effect your change in behavior will have on your father. The first chance you get, make sure you write down what happens so that you can report back to us in detail next session."

Now, it's time for you to carry out an experiment of your own at home. This experiment will give you practice in using the strategies of ***Pressing Your Own Buttons***™ for controlling troublesome social stimuli. If you repeat the seven steps frequently enough, you will soon notice a change in your behavior. As you do Steps 1 through 4, you'll become less tense. You'll feel less like changing or avoiding your troublesome situation. You'll become more relaxed. What is more, you'll learn to tolerate your troublesome stimulus.

As you do **Steps 5** through **7**, you'll learn to act differently. When you do, you'll also be able to choose your reaction. When you can *choose* your reaction, you act more freely. At this stage, however, the stimulus controls you. After doing **Steps 1** through **7** several times, you'll be in control. Before long, you'll be able to say you, ***"Take control of your life so others don't***™"

In the next chapter, I'm going to show you a completely new way of looking at your feelings and emotions.

Chapter 8:

Feelings, Emotions, and Actions

Let's explore our understanding of emotions and feelings. Before I

explain what I believe feelings and emotions are it's useful to consider your perspective on this. Before going on, take out a few pieces of paper and a pencil or pen. Then write your answers to the following questions. Doing so at this point is very important. I urge you, as I have before, do not go on until you have answered these questions in writing. Move on only when you have finished this bit of "homework."

1. What do you think emotions are?

NOTE: For the remaining two questions, you may wish to focus on just one specific "emotion." For example, substitute "anger," or "sadness" for "emotions."

1. How do your emotions affect you?

2. How do you handle, or deal with, your emotions?

Like most of us, you already have some ideas about emotions. You may even have some ideas about how emotions come about and how they affect you. Now, I'm going to tell you some new things about emotions and about how emotions relate to what we do. For you, this may be a completely new way of looking at emotions. To help in your understanding of this new approach to feeling and emotions, let's again join the Pressing Your Own Buttons™ group as they discuss emotions and how they're related to actions.

> Sigmund appeared quite relaxed. He smiled slightly as he began the session. "Today, we're going to talk about emotions and how emotions are related to actions. In this session, you're going to learn how emotions relate to what you do.
>
> "I'm sure you all have some thoughts about emotions already. You may even have some ideas about how emotions come about, and how they affect you. So, let's start by having you tell me what you think emotions are. How do you think they affect you, and how should we deal with them? Who'd like to start?" Sigmund waited as some of the participants squirmed nervously in their seats. Jayden appeared to be ready to respond but hesitated to be first. Taking this as a sign that the usually quite young man had some ideas to share, Sigmund called on him, "Jayden?"
>
> Tilting forward in his seat, Jayden responded thoughtfully, "I think emotions are physical feelings … like we get when we have certain thoughts … or when we find ourselves in certain situations."

- SMILING -

(POINTING FINGER)

- COMMANDING -

- LAUGHING -

Sigmund encouraged him to continue, "Tell me more about what you mean by, 'feelings we get when we have certain thoughts.'"

Jayden paused long enough to digest the question and form his answer, "Well ... when I see a beautiful girl, for example," he smiled as he spoke, "well ... I get a tight feeling in my stomach and sometimes my heart beats faster. That feeling might be love ... or, even lust!"

"Knowing you, it's lust," Renatta teased. Everyone, including Jayden, laughed. Her comment seemed to allow everyone to relax a little.

Sigmund probed further, "And the sensations you get ... which you say are signs of love or lust ... these are emotions, then? Is that right?"

Jayden thought for a moment then answered, "No. More like the *responses* to our thoughts or to the situations ... what I feel like doing!" Jayden's eyes sparkled as he reflected upon this insight.

"Thank you, Jayden. What do you think emotions are ... Martha?"

Martha sat straighter in her chair. She seemed caught off guard by Sigmund's question. Even so, she gave a carefully reasoned reply, "Well ... I think emotions are control mechanisms. They have a sense of good and bad about them. I think our emotions control what we do."

"How's that?" Sigmund asked as he encouraged Martha to continue her train of thought.

"Well … if I feel angry, for instance, I might want to hit you."

"Just try it," Sigmund said jokingly." Everyone laughed.

After a moment, Martha continued, "Anger is an emotion. And, when I'm angry it makes me want to fight."

"That's interesting Martha, thank you. Anyone else?"

A hand went up. "Yes, Jan."

"I think emotions are what we feel inside because of something that happens outside our bodies."

"You mean if I see someone gets hurt, I might be sad?"

"Yes. But, sometimes we don't like our emotions," Jan added.

Sigmund probed deeper, "Will you explain that further for us?"

Jan pulled her thoughts together as she formed her response, "Well … if … like Jayden … I saw someone who turned me on, and I knew he was married or something … I might feel guilty … I might want to get rid of, or deny that feeling. I mean … I might want to run up and hug him, but I know I shouldn't so I might do something to get rid of that feeling."

"You mean like take a cold shower?" Jayden added in jest.

Again, everyone laughed.

After a moment, Sigmund turned from his questioning of Jan to address the whole group, "Let me ask you, then, how do you think emotions affect us? … Cathy."

Cathy leaned toward the counselor as she replied, "I think emotions affect the way we see things, and the way we do things. For example, when I'm angry, I shout at people that bother me. However, when I'm sad, I want to be left alone. Like when my car wouldn't start last week and I was late for work. I got so mad that when I went into the house again, I slammed the door so hard the glass broke."

"In other words," Sigmund summed up, "Your anger expressed itself in your slamming the door? Is that right?"

"Uhuh ... and in my shouting at the car dealer when I phoned him about the broken starter in my car."

"How should we deal with our emotions, then?" Sigmund challenged the group to think on what Cathy had just said. Then, after a pause to allow the group to consider the question, he turned to Phil. "Can you help us, Phil?"

"I know it's not supposed to be a 'guy' thing to do ... but ... I think we have to express our feelings and emotions. We shouldn't keep stuff inside." Cathy, Renatta, and Margaret nodded in agreement with Phil's answer.

Again, Sigmund challenged the group, "If we're angry we should show it?"

Margaret replied with an emphatic, "Yes!"

However, it was Cathy, who elaborated. "I think we need to accept our emotions ... but ... I think we have to be careful how we express them."

"You don't think slamming the door or shouting was helpful then?" Sigmund asked.

Cathy responded with little hesitation, "No ... not really."

"But, didn't you have a right to be angry?" the counselor continued.

Again, Cathy spoke without hesitation, "You bet! But, yelling only got the dealer upset, and it wasn't really his fault."

Jan, uneasy with this answer, spoke out immediately, "Sure! You can't just do whatever you feel like because you're angry … We have to control our emotions."

Sigmund noticed this and, turning to Jan, asked her, "What do you mean?"

"Well," Jan elaborated, "we can't always do much about feeling angry. However, we can control the way we handle our anger."

"Do you agree with that, Alonzo?" Sigmund asked.

"Some. I think we learn as kids how to express our emotions … and … as we grow up, the way we act may or may not change. The problem comes when we don't handle our emotions the way society says we should. Then we get into trouble. You can't just do what you want just because you feel like it." Alonzo's reply seemed to sum up for the whole group.

"I take it from what you've said, then," said Sigmund as he continued to address the group, "most of you believe that emotions are somehow aroused in you and then these emotions *cause* you to do certain things.

"I also noted that many of you consider certain emotions to be unpleasant . . . something to get rid of. Most of you are also implying that if you are to change your behavior, it is first necessary to change your emotions and that different emotions will cause different behavior. That seems logical enough, doesn't it?

63

"You also seem to be saying that emotions are important … that you should pay attention to them.

"Now I think I understand your theory of emotions. It' seems plausible. In fact, it's the view held by most people. However, I want to suggest to you, it's also wrong."

The members of the group looked questioningly at each other. They seemed quite unprepared for Sigmund's last remark. Even so he continued, "I suggest that an almost opposite theory of emotions is more correct." Sigmund paused long enough for the group to begin to digest what he had just said. Then he continued, "Before I explain this further, I want to make something very clear. Indeed, emotions do feel either good or bad. It's good to have emotions. In fact, I suggest, it's good to have a wide variety of feelings or emotions. However, emotions are not as important in causing behavior as you think.

"Rather, what we *do* makes us feel the way we feel. If you want to feel differently, or have a different emotional experience, you must first *act* differently. This may not make sense to you at first, but as we talk about it more, and as you experiment with it, it will come to make very good sense." At that, Sigmund called for a short break.

When the group had gathered in their circle again, Sigmund returned to his earlier line of thought, "You'll remember from before, that when you're exposed to a stimulus, your first reaction is to evaluate whether it's good or bad. The evaluation you make produces an ***action tendency*** in you. You experience this action tendency as an emotion. The particular action tendency that is set up in you determines your emotional experience, not the other way around.

"Right now, you may be puzzled by the idea of action tendency. So, let me explain that further. By action tendency, I don't mean an action that you can see. Rather, an action tendency is a real physical feeling of action. An action tendency involves muscle activity that you can sense, but others may be unable to observe. It's a feeling of doing something but not necessarily doing it. It's not like observing you doing something or imagining yourself doing something. Rather, an action tendency is something you sense in your muscles.

"For example, suppose someone criticizes you. That person's criticizing you is a social stimulus. Now, let's suppose that you evaluate criticism as bad or dreadful. Your evaluation may set up an action tendency of getting away from the person criticizing you. On the other hand, you may experience an action tendency to change the person criticizing you. You may want to shout at them—even hit them! On the other hand, you may experience an action tendency to freeze up or to become tense in the presence of the criticism.

"The action tendency to get away will make you feel some emotion that you might call, 'fear.' The action tendency to change the person criticizing you might make you feel the emotion you label 'anger.' On the other hand, with the action tendencies to tense, freeze, or to avoid the situation altogether, you might call yourself 'anxious.'

"Suppose, for example, that you evaluated the same social stimulus—criticism—differently. Suppose you evaluated the criticism as an ordinary thing: something you would expect when you're just learning to do something better. Then, a different action tendency would occur and you would feel differently. Does that make sense?"

Everyone sat quietly, as each reflected on what Sigmund was saying. Some seemed puzzled, but none spoke as they considered the counselor's theory of emotions.

"Let's consider a more pleasant example," Sigmund continued to explain, "Suppose you were exposed to a good looking, charming, warm, and affectionate person. Isn't it quite possible that you would evaluate the stimuli as something positive and good? Such an evaluation could then lead to action tendencies of approaching, touching, and so forth. The accompanying emotional experience would likely feel good and be labeled as 'joy,' 'excitement,' or even 'love.'"

Everyone listened intently as Sigmund continued to clarify. "Let's look at the implications of this line of argument. What this theory of emotions says is, 'If you want to change your emotions or feelings, you'll first have to change your actions or action tendencies.' However, if you want to change your action tendencies, it will be necessary for you to first change your appraisal or evaluation of the social stimulus.

"It's for this very reason that I devoted a whole session to reappraising or re-evaluating the troublesome social stimuli that you identified earlier." They looked at each other knowingly.

"The theory I have outlined also says that it's a good idea to go ahead and deliberately try something different to see how it will make you feel. What is more, the theory is very clear. Focusing on, and becoming preoccupied with, your emotions will not help you change those emotions. Focusing on, and becoming preoccupied with, your emotions will not help you change your behavior either. However, if you vary your behavior and action tendencies, you'll experience a greater variety of emotions." On that note, Sigmund ended his explanation of this new perspective on emotions and action tendencies.

By now, you've become aware that facial expressions are important in influencing your behavior. The muscles of your face influence the emotions you experience. In fact, specific facial patterns are associated with specific emotional experiences. This means that the more facial expressions you have the more emotional experiences you'll have. Just look at these pictures and you'll see what I mean.

There is another point I must mention. It's concerned with how we interpret internal sensations. A few years ago, a psychologist did some interesting research. He found that the interpretations or labeling of bodily sensations determined our emotional expressions. He arranged it so that identical sensations were aroused in a group of people. Then, he got some of the people to think that the sensations were joyful. These people acted in a joyful manner. The researcher led the other people in the experiment to believe that the sensations were anger. These people acted in an angry manner.

In our work with people, we have found that they often misinterpret or mislabel their bodily sensations. I remember one young man who had certain sensations in his stomach. These sensations, he interpreted as "anxiety" or "going crazy." While he believed he <u>was</u> going crazy, he was only **interpreting** and **labeling** those sensations as, "I'm going crazy."

The More Facial Expressions, the More Emotional Experiences[10]

When I was able to show him that he had the same kinds of sensations when he was going up and down in an elevator, or when he was skiing down a hill, he felt much better about it.

 I've counseled people who thought certain sensations meant they were anxious when in fact they were sexually aroused. Interpreting or labeling internal sensations, is similar to the notion discussed earlier: making inferences.

Let's take some time now to consider what you think of this view of emotions. It would be particularly helpful if you could think of a personal experience that would illustrate what we've been talking about. For example, have you noticed that whenever you have acted differently you also have felt differently? Did you notice that the change in action came before, or preceded, the change in feeling? Have you ever changed your interpretation of some internal sensation after learning more about the situation that brought it about?

To further clarify what I've been saying let's see how the participants in the group handled these same questions.

> Sigmund began the new session. His tone was relaxed and comforting as he summarized the last meeting. "We have learned that when we are exposed to social stimuli, our first reaction is to evaluate them as either good or bad. The evaluation we then make produces an action tendency. This action tendency we experience as an emotion. We have also learned that it is not our emotions that determine our actions but our actions that determine our emotions. The evaluations we make of specific social stimuli produce action tendencies in us. These action tendencies we experience as emotions.

"In other words," he continued, "What we do, or tend to do, determines how we feel. Therefore, if we want to change our emotions, we first need to change our actions or action tendencies. Usually though … a change in our evaluation of a particular social stimulus is necessary before we will change our actions in response to it.

Turning now to involve the group directly, Sigmund asked, "Has anyone had an experience where a change in actions resulted in a change in emotions?"

"Yes, Dave."

A little hesitant at first, Dave offered his response, "I once tried an experiment where I work."

"Would you tell us about it?" Sigmund invited encouragingly.

"Well," Dave continued, "I decided that I was fed up with the Gloomy Gusses at the office. I had just read an article on how our smiling causes others to smile. So, I decided to act differently when I came to work the next day. As I arrived, the door attendant met me. Right away—and I don't usually do this—I said smilingly, 'Good morning. How are you today?'

"The doorman seemed surprised but smiled and said, 'Good morning,' right back. That's not surprising I know. But, then he also asked how I was. Ordinarily, I'd say 'fine.' That day, though, I said, 'Fantastic!' and smiled back at him. I did the same thing with everyone I met. You know, before long, lots of people were smiling around the office and I felt terrific myself. That was a big change from the way I usually feel."

"Thanks, Dave," Sigmund said enthusiastically, "That's an excellent example of what we mean when we say your actions affect your emotions. Tell me, Dave, when you started out that day, did you really feel, as you said, 'Fantastic!'?"

69

Dave responded without hesitation, "No. I really didn't. In fact I was skeptical about whether my experiment would work at all."

"So, your change in feelings or emotions came *after* you changed your actions, not before. Is that right?"

"Yes, absolutely! I only felt fantastic after a few people smiled back at me and seemed cheerful."

All was quiet for a time before Sigmund continued. "Does anyone recall a situation in which they changed their interpretation of some internal sensation they experienced?"

Margaret responded immediately, "I have."

"Would you share that experience with us?" Sigmund encouraged her.

"Well," Margaret continued, "I used to get this feeling in my stomach whenever my brother wouldn't listen to me or do as I asked when I looked after him. I used to get the same tight feeling in my stomach when my dad got angry with my mom or us. My stomach would be very tense and so would my arms. I always thought of this as fear or anger."

A light came on in Sigmund's head as he considered Margaret's comments in past sessions and those she made here. "You seem to feel that giving orders or being ignored is a bad, even horrid, thing. Is that right, Margaret?"

Margaret seemed surprised as she considered the counselor's question. "I used to." She answered, "But, when I tried some of the experiments you suggested in the group, I began to feel differently. One time I pictured my dad in a cage when he was yelling at my younger brother. I pictured myself conducting my father's yelling ... like a conductor leads an orchestra. Instead of leaving the room when my stomach felt tense, I mentally told myself that the tightness in my stomach was excitement over conducting my father 'singing.'

"This may sound weird, but I actually began to feel less tense. And as I did this more often, I no longer felt I had to leave the room. Now, I think I can see my dad's yelling as his problem, not mine. In fact, I believe I think of yelling as not so bad at all. Certainly my dad's yelling hasn't killed anyone, and he gets over it before long anyway."

"Very good, Margaret." Sigmund continued without a break, "You not only changed your interpretation of your father's yelling, but you also changed your own actions in the presence of this social stimulus. Your change in actions has caused a change in your feelings about your father's yelling. Clearly, too, your changed interpretation, your re-evaluation if you will, of the stimulus yelling, made it easier for you to change your reactions to your father's yelling.

"Thank you for sharing that with us."

As you can see, our **reappraisal** of a **troublesome social stimulus** opens the way for a change in our actions or action tendencies. Whenever we change our actions or action tendencies, we wind up changing our emotions.

In the next chapter, we we're going to look at another kind of stimuli that can affect our behavior.

Chapter 9:

The "Hot Buttons" Within

What you'll discover in this chapter may be the most difficult to learn so far. However, you've already done so well learning how to deal with your own troublesome social stimuli. Therefore, I'm very confident you'll learn this new material, too. One good thing about a book, you can read any part over again as often as you like.

In earlier chapters, we paid a great deal of attention to **external social stimuli**. There you learned the effects they can have on your behavior. You'll recall that we looked at how we evaluate, and react to, external stimuli. We noted how particular external social stimuli could have interfering or controlling effects on our behavior. We also discussed and experienced ways of changing your evaluations and reactions. As you did so, you became more comfortable with external social stimuli and less controlled by them. The behavior of others need no longer control you. You are free to act as you choose.

Now I want to tell you about another kind of social stimuli that can affect your behavior: your **internal stimuli**. There are two distinct types of internal stimuli. The first are **internal sensations**. The second are **response tendencies**. I'll deal with them separately in order to make a clear distinction between them. These ideas may seem somewhat confusing at first. Don't get too concerned about that. It's quite normal. Please be patient. You'll soon understand these new ideas.

Let's start with internal sensations. They are internal bodily stimuli—actual physical sensations inside your body—such as increased heart rate, muscle twitches, trembling, "knots" or "butterflies" in your stomach, and so forth. These sensations are sometimes localized and specific, such as when your heart rate increases. At other times, internal sensations can be diffused, vague, and rather generalized sensations.

To focus more clearly on what I mean, make a chart like the one in **Appendix D**, then, complete the following short exercise:

1. In the first column of the chart, list some internal bodily sensations that you've had. List as many as you can recall having experienced.

2. In either the second column, or the third column, whichever is most appropriate, indicate with an X whether each is good or bad.

3. In whichever of the remaining columns—4, 5, 6, or 7—is most appropriate, indicate with an X whether you try to avoid, change, or tense in the presence of the stimulus, or whether you simply ignore it.

Internal sensations are like external social stimuli. What is more, just like external social stimuli, for some people internal sensations can be just as troublesome and aversive. For them, internal stimuli can prove just as controlling as external social stimuli. For such people, whenever they feel a certain internal sensation, they will usually make an effort to stop it. Trying to stop the internal sensations can interfere with that individual's normal patterns. Doing so may even have an incapacitating effect on that person.

More specifically, the problem comes if you focus your attention too much on an internal sensation. When you direct all your efforts at changing or terminating the internal sensation, then you stop yourself from learning new ways of coping with important **external social stimuli**. For example, consider what would happen if, every time you asked an employer about a job, you noticed a tight knot in your stomach. Now suppose you had learned to evaluate that knot in your stomach as very unpleasant. Then you would try hard to get rid of the sensation, wouldn't you? You would probably work very hard to get rid of that knot.

Unfortunately, so much effort directed at the knot in your stomach, might lead to you being as brief as possible with the potential employer. In time, you might avoid talking to the employer altogether. You might even behave in some other less effective manner. In any case, your preoccupation with that internal sensation—like the knot in your stomach— could lead to your not being hired. Yet, you might be well qualified to do the job.

Clearly, a preoccupation with internal sensations could greatly limit your freedom to deal effectively with other people.

Take a few minutes now to get a pencil or pen, and a sheet of paper.

Do you have the pen and paper? Great! Now, I want you to write down some examples of internal sensations from your *own* experience. List the internal sensations that you find unpleasant. List only those you try to change or avoid. When you've finished, continue with the chapter.

View internal sensations in much the same way I showed you how to look at external social stimuli. You handle both in much the same way. Reappraise any internal sensation that is troublesome, just as you would reappraise a troublesome external social stimulus. You can also desensitize yourself to it, just as you can in the case of external social stimuli.

Let's see how Sigmund demonstrates this procedure with the group.

"Could I have a volunteer who experiences some difficulty with an internal sensation, to help me with a demonstration?" he asked, pausing for a response. "Yes ... Paul."

"Paul, I want you to try to recall a situation in which you experienced the troublesome internal sensation. Try to imagine the situation as concretely and as vividly as possible. Recall the internal sensations that you found troublesome. What do you feel?"

Leaning forward in his chair Paul offered his situation for consideration. "I feel a tight knot in my stomach, like somebody's fist is there."

"Thank you. Now, try to maintain that knot in your stomach. Don't try to change it. Instead ... I want you to focus on it and describe in more detail what it feels like."

"It's a very tight feeling in the pit of my stomach." Paul shifted uncomfortably in his chair as his stomach muscles tightened noticeably. "It's almost like a cramp. Actually, it feels awful. I don't like it." Again, Paul shifted his body as he sat further back in his seat.

"Just focus on it again ... briefly. See whether it really is that bad. Are you in real pain? Can you still walk and talk? Does it really hurt you or incapacitate you?" Sigmund probed deeper into Paul's experience of this internal stimulus.

Relaxing only slightly, Paul replied. His voice still showed signs of the discomfort he felt. "Well ... no ... it doesn't hurt terribly ... but, I sure don't like it!"

"Focus on it again. Is it any worse than having a slight case of indigestion?"

At first, Paul seemed confused by the question. When he did understand, he continued to explain, "I don't know ... I don't think so ... I guess not."

"Again, Paul," Sigmund persisted, "really try to make a deliberate effort to maintain the sensation. Notice what it feels like. Only now, try to become used to it. Try to picture it as just a little tightness in your stomach that won't really hurt you. Believe that as you become used to it, you'll find that it isn't as unpleasant as you thought it would be.

"Now, Paul, although I'm asking you to focus on the sensation, it is important to remember that the goal of this procedure is to make you more comfortable with the internal sensation. In time, you'll not focus on it so much. I want you to direct your attention away from the internal sensation. The idea is to get your attention redirected outwards toward coping with external social stimuli. If you can tolerate the internal sensation you'll be able to focus on the external social stimulus that leads you to respond this way." With that, Sigmund left Paul and the others to reflect upon what they had just experienced.

The same procedure the counselor used here with Paul, you can use also. Dealing with your negative reactions to certain internal sensations by focusing on the external social stimulus that causes them will lead to a more effective response on your part.

For example, if you sometimes get a knot in the pit of your stomach, and if that sensation upsets you, you might want to use this procedure to handle the problem. However, use this approach only—and I stress <u>only</u>—if the internal sensation, like a knot in your stomach, interferes with your acting freely with external social stimuli. Otherwise, ignore it and concentrate on dealing with the external stimulus instead.

Let me stress never, never, *never* use this procedure if the internal sensations <u>do not</u> make you tense or if you don't feel compelled to change or avoid them. Never use this procedure, unless you <u>must</u> get away from the external stimuli associated with the internal sensations. It isn't necessary—in fact it's undesirable—to become preoccupied with your internal sensations. Paying too much attention to all the little sensations that go on in your body all the time will make you less attentive to external social stimuli. Moreover, doing so will also make you less effective in dealing with those troublesome external stimuli. Contrary to what the famous emperor said in Shakespeare's *Julius Caesar,* "The fault, dear Brutus, is not in our stars but in ourselves, that we are underlings."[11] In this case, the problem is *not* inside. The real source of your concern is the *external* social stimulus: the thing another person does that presses our buttons. It's outside you! That said, if you do find a certain internal sensation to be interfering, or troublesome, you can do the following:

1. Try to maintain the sensation. Do not suppress it when it occurs in a real setting.

2. Try to focus on the sensation and note whether it really is so unpleasant. Pay attention to what the sensation consists of. Notice whether it hurts to try to appraise it more accurately and appropriately.

3. Try to become more used to the sensation. At the same time, become aware that it may not be as unpleasant as you had assumed it would be.

At this point, I suggest you take some time to digest these new ideas. Set the book aside for a day or so. Then return to it. You may at that time want to reread the above material. That's a good idea. For now, put the book down and return to it later when you are ready to continue reading.

Response Tendencies

The second category of internal stimuli, that can have interfering effects on behavior for a small number of individuals, is response tendencies. Although these stimuli are also internal, they are different from internal sensations. Consider this:

1. Internal sensations *are - vague, diffused, general patterns of sensations.*

2. Response tendencies *are - organized tendencies to respond.*

Take a moment to reread numbers 1 and 2 above. Be sure you see the distinction. Understanding the difference between internal sensations and response tendencies is important if you are to understand what follows below.

Two common response tendencies are those of anger and affection. In each case, the response tendency consists of a sense of wanting to do something specific. For some individuals, the external social stimulus does not cause the difficulty directly. Instead, the external stimulus can elicit a response tendency that they may only then attempt to suppress. Doing so, however, can interfere with their functioning effectively. This is because you can appraise response tendencies—as with external stimuli—as negative or aversive and you may feel compelled to change or avoid them.

For example, when we are growing up, we can place negative emphasis on getting angry or acting in an affectionate way. Then, we may negatively appraise the associated response tendencies as bad or—more technically—as aversive. Unfortunately, people often believe that having a response tendency also means they will automatically act on it. This belief is wrong. Just because people "feel" angry, doesn't mean they have to act in an angry way. Just

78

because they "feel" affectionate toward another person, doesn't mean they have to act in an affectionate way. We can all have many kinds of response tendencies without acting on them inappropriately in a given situation.

Just as with external social stimuli and internal sensations (our button pressers), it is possible to become more comfortable with response tendencies (our emotions). We can have response tendencies without acting upon them. You'll see how this is possible as Sigmund works with a volunteer from the group.

In this last example, the counselor deals with a situation in which a young woman, Pat, feels uncomfortable with Aaron, a male friend of her brother. Pat feels uncomfortable in the presence of Aaron because Pat also has thoughts of wanting to be affectionate with him. She has a response tendency of affection towards her brother's friend. Pat needs to understand that a desire to act in an affectionate way does not mean she must act in an affectionate way. At this point, Pat fears she might act inappropriately.

> "Pat," Sigmund spoke softly as he directed his attentions to the young woman seated across from him. "I'd like you to recall a situation in which you felt uncomfortable in the presence of your brother's friend. Try to recall the situation as concretely as you can. Experience the feelings you did then. Can you do that?" He waited for a response.

> After some consideration, and unsure whether she really wanted to discuss this problem at this time, Pat decided to press ahead. This was a very real issue with her and she wanted to know how to deal with it more effectively than she had been able to do. "Well ... sort of ... but not quite as strongly as I did in the actual situation."

> "That's fine," Sigmund encouraged her to continue, "For now, just try to maintain the feeling."

Pat was noticeably uncomfortable with the scenario. With her arms folded across her chest, she shuffled her feet, and repositioned herself against the back of her chair. After a moment or two of reflection, she began to relax and placed her hands in her lap. "I don't like to do that."

Aware of her discomfort, Sigmund prodded her gently. "Just try briefly. Try to be alert to the first feeling you experience and differentiate that from your reaction to the feeling. Let's focus briefly … perhaps with your eyes shut if that helps focus on the first feeling … and let's see whether it is unpleasant at all."

"As I imagine my brother's friend," Pat pressed on, "I can see him standing by the refrigerator. I have tightness in my stomach as I picture him standing there, and my heart is pounding. I don't like the feelings I have."

"Is it possible that it is your evaluation of it that makes it unpleasant?" Sigmund probed gently.

"I guess it's possible." Pat seemed skeptical but was clearly willing to pursue this line of thought further.

"I suggest to you that it's *very* possible," Sigmund was relaxed but firm in his conviction. "Now, as you experience the situation as concretely as you can, picture again how you were feeling inside at the time. Only this time try to consider the possibility that it really is pleasant."

"It isn't unpleasant," Pat assured him, "But, then, it isn't completely real ... I don't feel exactly as I did then in the actual situation."

"We can still focus on it here a few more times; pay particular attention to whether it really is unpleasant. Now, visualize your brother's friend at the refrigerator again. Recall the tightness in your stomach. Do you recall what you felt like doing at the time?"

Hesitating at first, Pat continued to describe her experience, "No ...well ... yes, actually I guess I felt like I wanted to hug him. I hardly knew him. Why would I hug him?"

"You believe that hugging him would have been inappropriate. Is that right?"

Sitting forward in her seat and making her pronouncement quite emphatically, Pat replied emphatically, "I can't just run up and hug every guy I see!"

Sigmund smiled, as he nodded in agreement, "No, Pat, that wouldn't be appropriate." Then, turning to the others he continued, "I want to emphasize here and now, that the most beneficial way to deal with any response tendency is in the actual situation."

That said, Sigmund again turned his attention to Pat. "Pat, for now I want you to continue to visualize the situation here and now. However, now I want you to try to be alert to when the response tendency comes up in real-life settings. Then, make a deliberate effort to maintain it as long as you possibly can."

Pat hesitated. "But, what if I really act on the feeling? What if I really do go up and hug Aaron? What if I show him affection? I'd die of embarrassment!"

Sigmund spoke calmly and confidently, "Pat, I understand what you're saying ... Let me assure you that doesn't need to happen. You can have all kinds of feelings and urges without ever acting on them. You can become completely comfortable with your response tendencies and still only express them or act on them when the situation is appropriate."

Pat was clearly more comfortable with this, "You mean the feeling I have is an action tendency ... that affection is an action tendency? You mean … I'm uncomfortable around Aaron because I really feel affectionate towards him. That I'm concerned that I might act affectionately?"

"Yes … absolutely! The sensation you feel is an action tendency of affection towards your brother's friend. At this time, you want to suppress that action tendency because you feel that right now it's not appropriate. However, because you *feel* affectionately towards your brother's friend, you don't have to fear that you'll *act* affectionately towards him in an inappropriate way.

"However," Sigmund smiled as he paused to collect his thoughts, "later, especially if your brother's friend shows some interest in you, you just might decide to be affectionate with him. At that time, your action tendency may be appropriate. For the present you can handle this stimulus as you do other controlling stimuli."

There, now you have a better understanding of internal sensations and response tendencies as well as of the difference between them. You've also learned some important strategies for dealing with them. Now, when confronted with either type of stimuli, you'll be able act freely in their presence.

In ***Pressing Your Own Buttons: Take Control of Your Life So Others Don't!***™, I have shown you how to identify troublesome social stimuli. I have also shown you how to reappraise them so that you can desensitize yourself to them. Now you can act more freely in the presence of other people.

Not every concept I've covered in the book will be clear to you at this time. As I said at the beginning of the chapter, you can always re-read any part of a book that you choose, and at any time you choose to.

I encourage you to go over those sections that may not be clear to you at this time. Rereading that material will help you understand it better.

Many of our clients have found the companion book, the ***Pressing Your Own Buttons Programmed Workbook***™, quite useful. The ***Programmed Workbook*** will prove very helpful in getting a solid handle on the concepts involved. It will also serve as an excellent review tool for those who already have a good understanding of the current book. Should you choose to do so, you can purchase the ***Programmed Workbook*** from the publisher.

Coming Soon!

Another option, coming soon, will be a **FREE** introductory session of our soon-to-be-completed *Pressing Your Own Buttons Teleseminar*™. Before long, you will be able to participate without even leaving the privacy of your home. For those who may be unfamiliar with the term "teleseminar," let me say simply that a teleseminar is like any other seminar with a group of interested participants, except this time the seminar is by telephone. You register, dial up the seminar number, and input the code we will give you when we confirm your registration. That's it!

Another trainer or I will take you one step at a time through the program and answer all your questions as you go along. You'll also be able to hear the questions and comments of the other participants. This is a powerful way in which to learn, and then master, the skills while addressing the specific "hot button" issues in your own life. To request more information about your **FREE** introductory session, go to http://www.garyscreatonpage.com.

Alternatively, you may choose to participate in one of our weekend *Pressing Your Own Buttons Boot Camps*™. These take place over two-day weekends in a hotel or resort setting. Boot Camps allow you to participate on a face-to-face basis with others who share your desire to *Press Your Own Buttons*™ and, *Take Control of Your Life So Others Don't!*™. Only the author, Gary Screaton Page, or a licensed Associate presents at the Boot Camps. At the time of writing this, we will be scheduling just two Boot Camps per year.

Enrollment for the teleseminars, as for our Bootcamps, will be limited. Be sure to indicate your interest early to ensure your place. For more information on any of these life-changing opportunities, go to our Web site Web site (www.garyscreatonpage.com) and look for updated information. Also, check out my Blog, which answers readers' questions, provides tips for living more fully, and offers many products and services that will help you ***"Take Control of Your Life So Others Don't!"***™

Remember, the more you review the material, and the more use you make of the other tools available to you, the more you'll find yourself able to act freely in the presence of other people. The old adage, "Practice makes perfect," is especially appropriate if you want to, ***"Take Control of Your Life So Others Don't!"***™. Whenever you feel unclear about some area of the material, turn to that part of the book, or workbook, and review it. I know you'll be a more effective person for having read the book and done the various activities.

Congratulations! You have already seen some big changes in your life. Remember, this book will always be here to help you in the future.

There you have it! Now, more than ever before, you can say with confidence you are ***Pressing Your Own Buttons***™. Now you really can ***"Take control of your life so others don't!"***™

- THE END -

Appendixes

A. Your Button Pressers

B. Discovering Your "Hot Buttons"

C. Seven Simple Steps to Personal Freedom™

D. The "Hot Buttons" Within

E. The "Hot Buttons" Within You

Appendix A

Your Button Pressers

Person	(1) Other's Behavior	(2) My Reactions	(3) Type of Reaction
Mother (Critical, Angry, Sad, Friendly, Commanding, Ignoring)			
Father (Critical, Angry, Sad, Friendly, Commanding, Ignoring)			
Teacher (Critical, Angry, Sad, Friendly, Commanding, Ignoring)			
Boss (Critical, Angry, Sad, Friendly, Commanding, Ignoring)			
Close Friend (Critical, Angry, Sad, Friendly, Commanding, Ignoring)			

Appendix B

Discovering Your "Hot Buttons"

SOCIAL STIMULI	PERSON	OWN REACTIONS
	E.g., Mother, Father, Teacher, Boss or Close Friend	E.g., What you did, said, sensations you experienced
Friendliness: friendly, smiling saying nice things	a b c	a b c
Anger: angry/ hostile	a b c	a b c
Sadness: sad, crying, frowning	a b c	a b c
Criticism: critical, disapproving, sarcastic	a b c	a b c
Ignoring: unresponsive, indifferent, does not pay attention	a b c	a b c
Commanding	a	a

ordering, demanding	b	b
	c	c
Impulsivity	a	a
Lively, exuberant, behaving impulsively	b	b
	c	c

Appendix C

Seven Simple Steps to Personal Freedom™

STEP 1: Imagine the stimulus. Get a clear picture of it.

STEP 2: Pretend you are a scientist looking at this situation. Remember: Write the <u>exact</u> words spoken. Describe <u>exactly</u> what you see, hear, and what others involved do.

STEP 3: Imagine the other person in a cage, surrounded by a hedge, behind an unbreakable glass barrier, etc. Imagine you are a scientist examining their behavior as they do their thing. At first, do so for just a few seconds then for longer and longer periods.

STEP 4: Now, more comfortable imagining the other person, picture yourself doing something different from what you usually do.

STEP 5: When the above situation comes up again, do STEPS 1 through 4, for real this time! At first, just look at the person. As this becomes easier, do STEP 4.

STEP 6: Reappraisal. What do they actually say, do, and look like? Chances are these things aren't so bad after all.

STEP 7: Where did you learn this evaluation? For example, what did your father do when he saw or heard this stimulus? How about your mother, teacher, boss, or close friend? What did they say, do? How did they look?

Appendix D

Seven Simple Steps to Personal Freedom™ Diagram

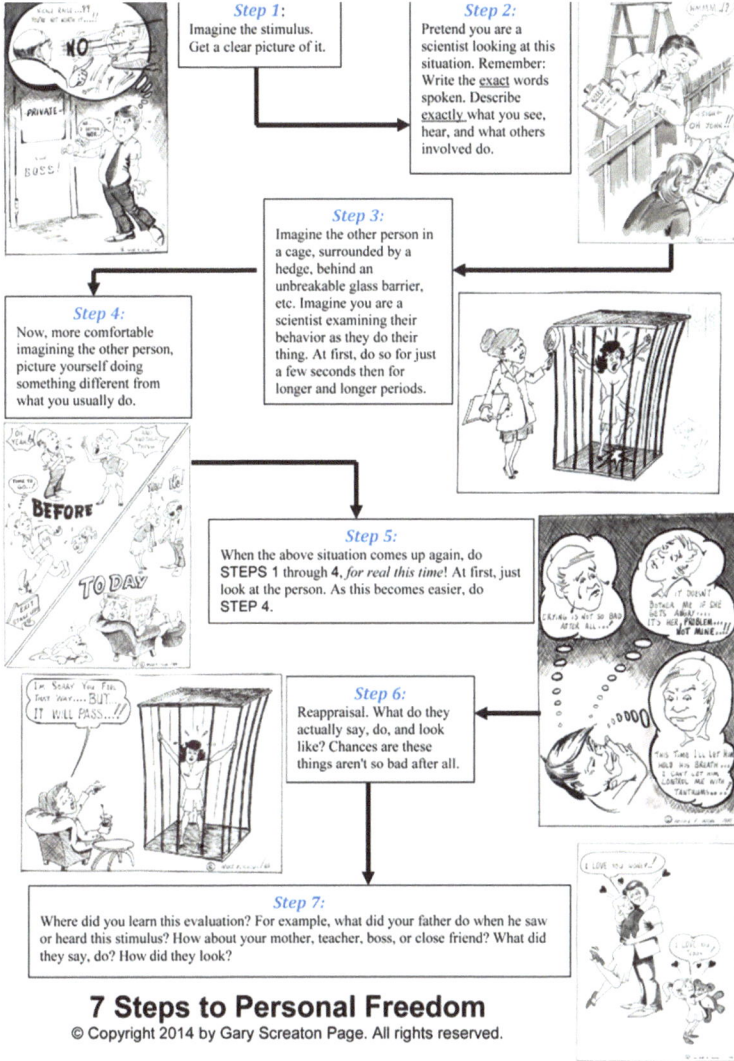

Step 1:
Imagine the stimulus. Get a clear picture of it.

Step 2:
Pretend you are a scientist looking at this situation. Remember: Write the exact words spoken. Describe exactly what you see, hear, and what others involved do.

Step 3:
Imagine the other person in a cage, surrounded by a hedge, behind an unbreakable glass barrier, etc. Imagine you are a scientist examining their behavior as they do their thing. At first, do so for just a few seconds then for longer and longer periods.

Step 4:
Now, more comfortable imagining the other person, picture yourself doing something different from what you usually do.

Step 5:
When the above situation comes up again, do STEPS 1 through 4, *for real this time*! At first, just look at the person. As this becomes easier, do STEP 4.

Step 6:
Reappraisal. What do they actually say, do, and look like? Chances are these things aren't so bad after all.

Step 7:
Where did you learn this evaluation? For example, what did your father do when he saw or heard this stimulus? How about your mother, teacher, boss, or close friend? What did they say, do? How did they look?

7 Steps to Personal Freedom

91

Appendix E

The "Hot Buttons" Within You

1	2	3	4	5	6	7
Internal Bodily Sensations I Have Had	Sensation Was Good	Sensation Was Bad	Avoid	Change	Tense	Ignore

About the Author

Gary Screaton Page, M.Ed., Ph.D., is a Pastor, award-winning educator, school counselor, author, speaker, seminar/workshop facilitator, counselor/therapist, and entrepreneur. For more than four decades, Gary taught and counselled students from primary grades through college and university. He also taught teachers and was Contributing Editor of The Educational Courier for the Ontario Teachers' Federation. Gary has been a Guidance Specialist since Jan. 1972, and was formerly Head of Guidance at Port Colborne High School with the Niagara District School Board. Gary was an educational consultant for children's television and appeared on several national television shows and has been heard on numerous radio stations throughout the world.

Gary Page conducts parenting workshops based on the skills in his book, *Being the Parent YOU Want to Be: 12 Communication Skills for Effective Parenting*. Dr. Page has created an online self-directed counselling course, *Pressing Your Own Buttons: Take control of Your Life So Others Don't!*™, and helped countless families improve their communication skills. He is a Deacon and retired Sr. Pastor of First Baptist Church-Fort Erie. He has a B.A. in Psychology, an M.Ed. in Sociology of Education, and a Ph.D. in Counselling. He has authored several books, written numerous articles on parenting, as well as written for educational publications. Inspector

Rev. Dr. Gary Screaton Page is a Service Chaplain with the Niagara Regional Police Service, a Member of the Boards of the Jericho House Youth Leadership, Justice, and Spirituality Centre (http://ww.jerichohouse.org) and the Matthew House Refugee Ministry in Fort Erie, ON, Canada (http://matthewhouseforterie.com/).

Books by
Gary Screaton, M.Ed., Ph.D.

- *Being the Parent YOU Want to Be: 12 Communication Skills for Effective Parenting*

- *Being the Parent YOU Want to Be: 12 Communication Skills for Effective Parenting Facilitator Guide*

- *Pressing Your Own Buttons: Take Control of Your Life So Others Don't!™*

- *100+ Unconditionally Guaranteed, Genuinely Easy, Success Strategies for Students*

Notes

[1] B. Bloch (Research Officer), and I. Briedis, R. Elsie, J. Heath, H. Shannon (Graduate Assistants).

[2] See footnote 1.

[3] Luciano L'Abate and Demian Goldstein (2007). Workbooks for the promotion of mental health and life-ling learning. In Luciano L'Abate (2007). *Low-Cost Approaches to Promote Physical and Mental Health*. New York: Springer *Science+Business* Media, pp 285-302. Among others.

[4] This eBook is **not** a **psychoanalytic** system, however. Rather, it is a social **interactional** approach to well-being.

[5] I suggest that we could call social stimuli "button pressers." Each troublesome social stimulus acts as a button presser that causes us to compulsively tense, avoid, or try to change that stimulus. It's as though the source person had pressed a button to make us react.

[6] The things that people say, do, or how they look that compel us to want to avoid or change them, or which cause us to tense in their presence.

[7] Wen Li, Isabel Moallem, Ken A. Paller, and Jay A. Gottfried (2007). Subliminal smells can guide social preferences. *Psychological Science, Volume 18, Number 12.* According to these authors, "social preferences are subject to influences from odors

that escape awareness, whereas the availability of conscious odor information may disrupt such effects." See their list of references included with their paper. Last viewed May 19, 2015 at http://labs.feinberg.northwestern.edu/gottfried/pdfs/li_gottfried_ps ychsci07.pdf.

[8] "Social Stimuli" refer to those things only a person says, does, or how they look. Only people can be sources of social stimuli. I will occasionally refer to "social stimuli" as "button pressers."

[9] This is to say, they give orders, make demands, or tell you what to do.

[10] I have had this picture in my files for many years. I've seen it many times elsewhere as well, always without the source being given. It is only proper that the originator receive credit for the work. It is not my intent to avoid giving proper credit. Upon notification and proof of origin, I will give proper credit in subsequent editions.

[11] William Shakespeare. *Julius Caesar*. Act i. Sc. 2.

www.ingramcontent.com/pod-product-compliance
Lightning Source LLC
Chambersburg PA
CBHW040512290326
41930CB00035B/2